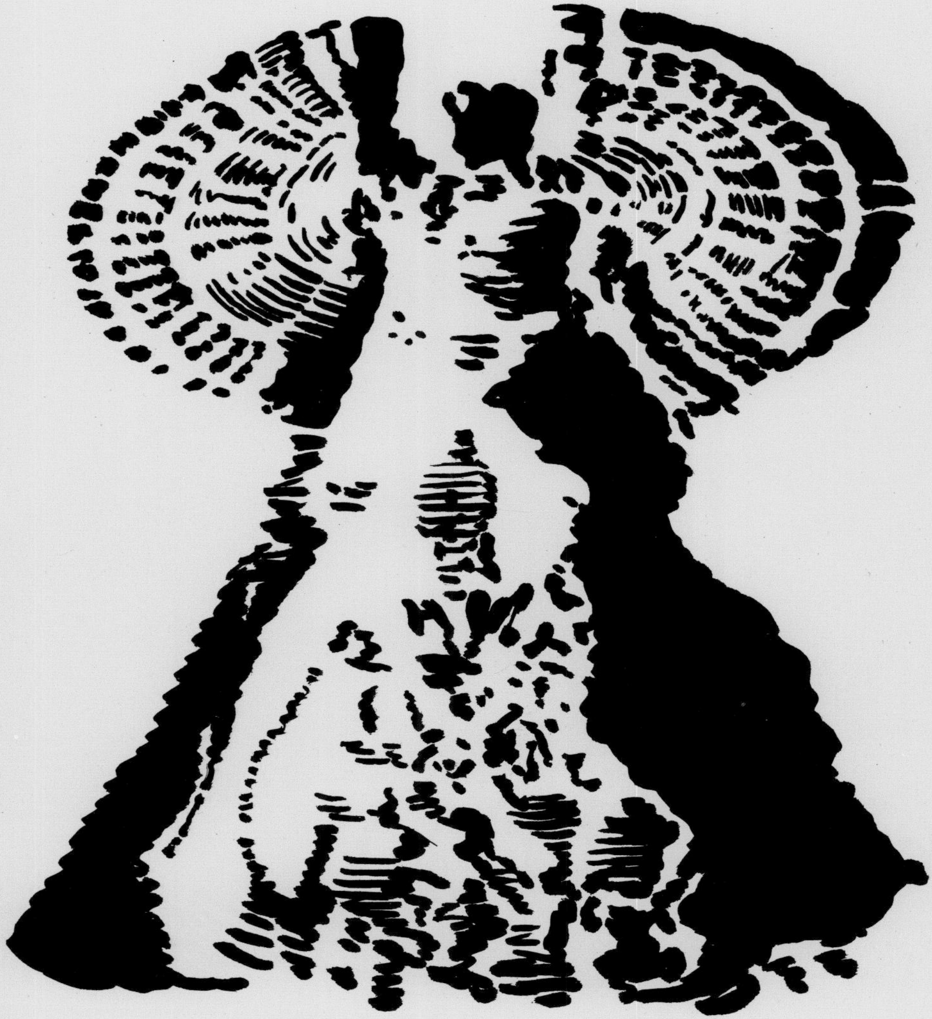

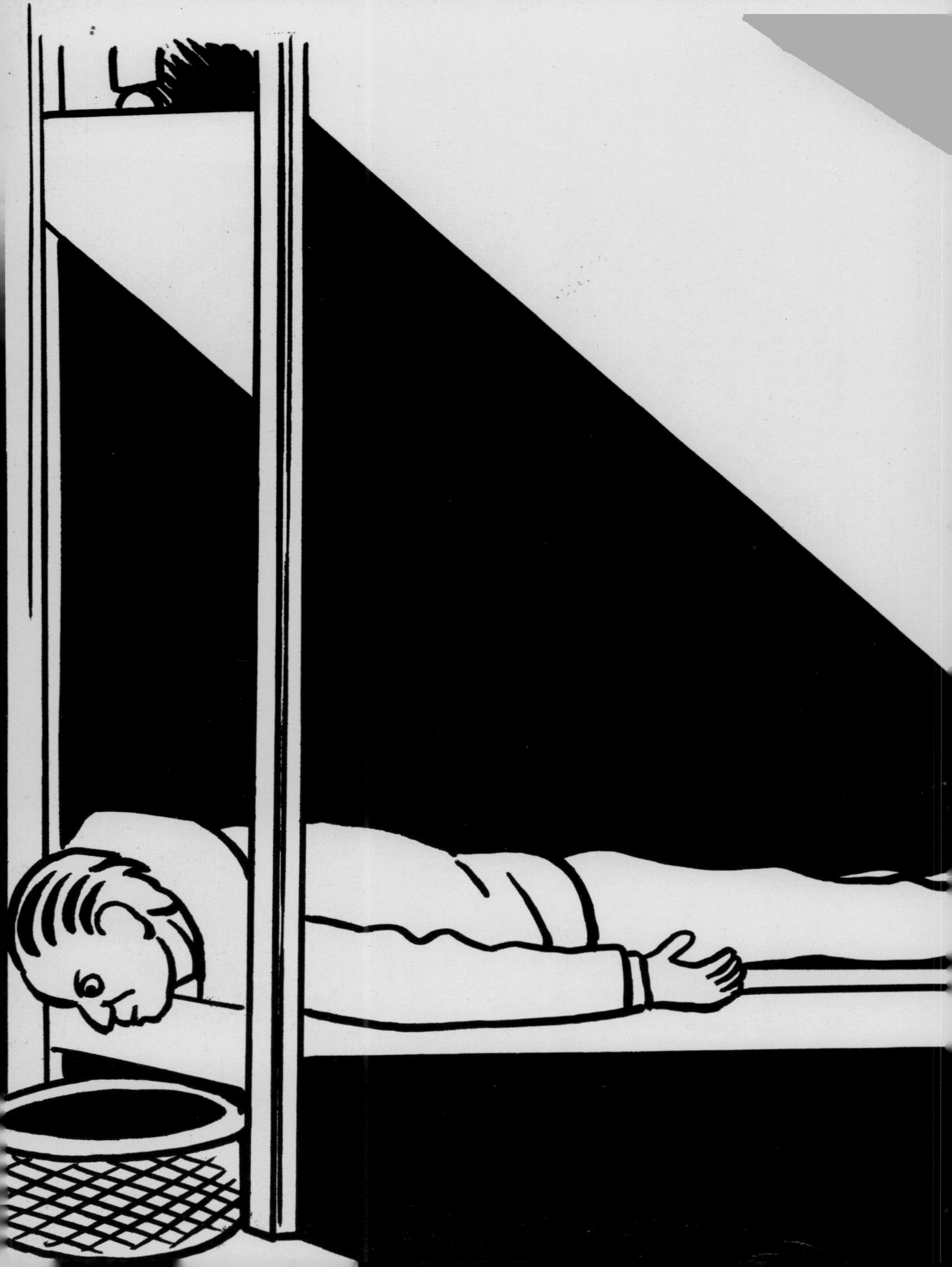

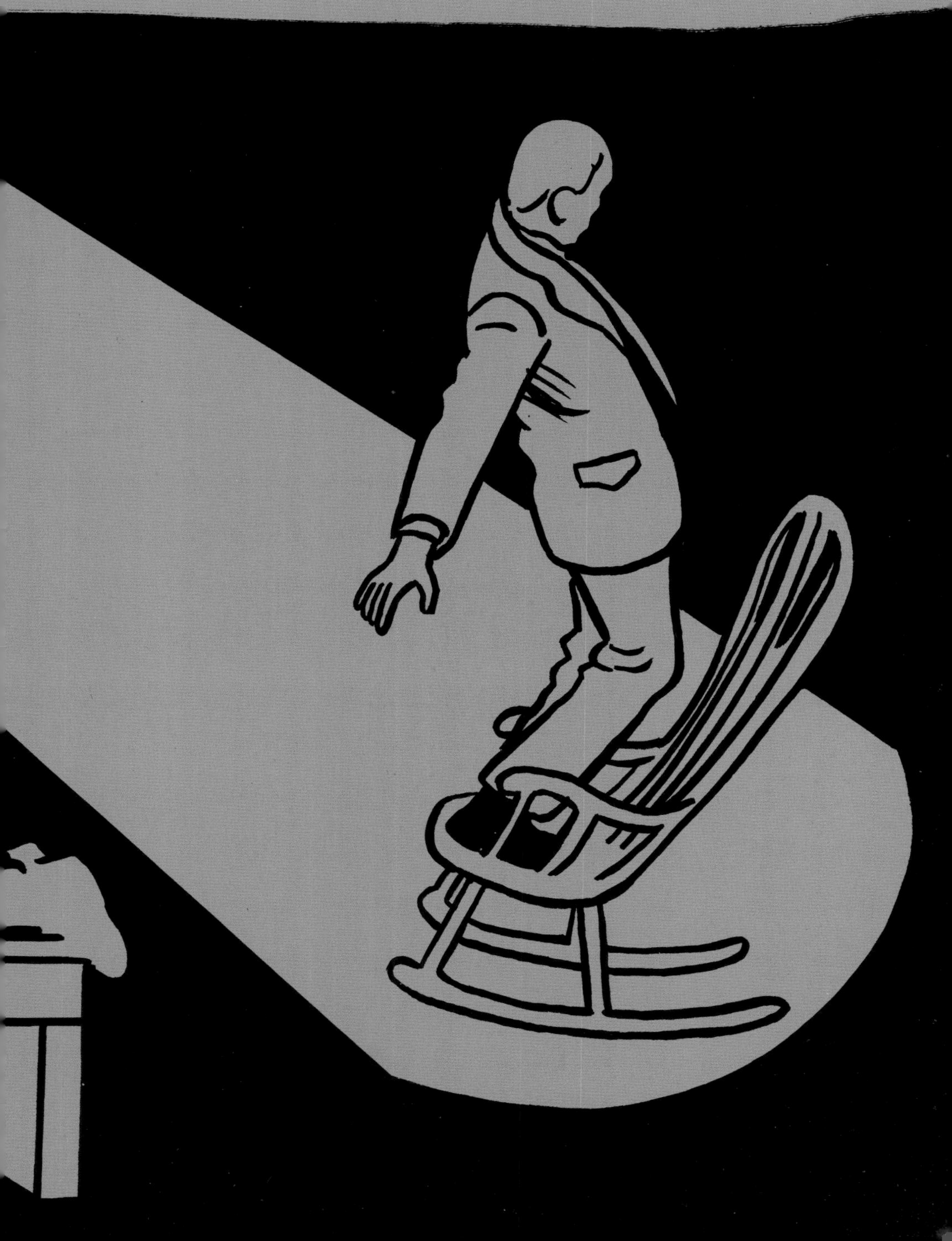

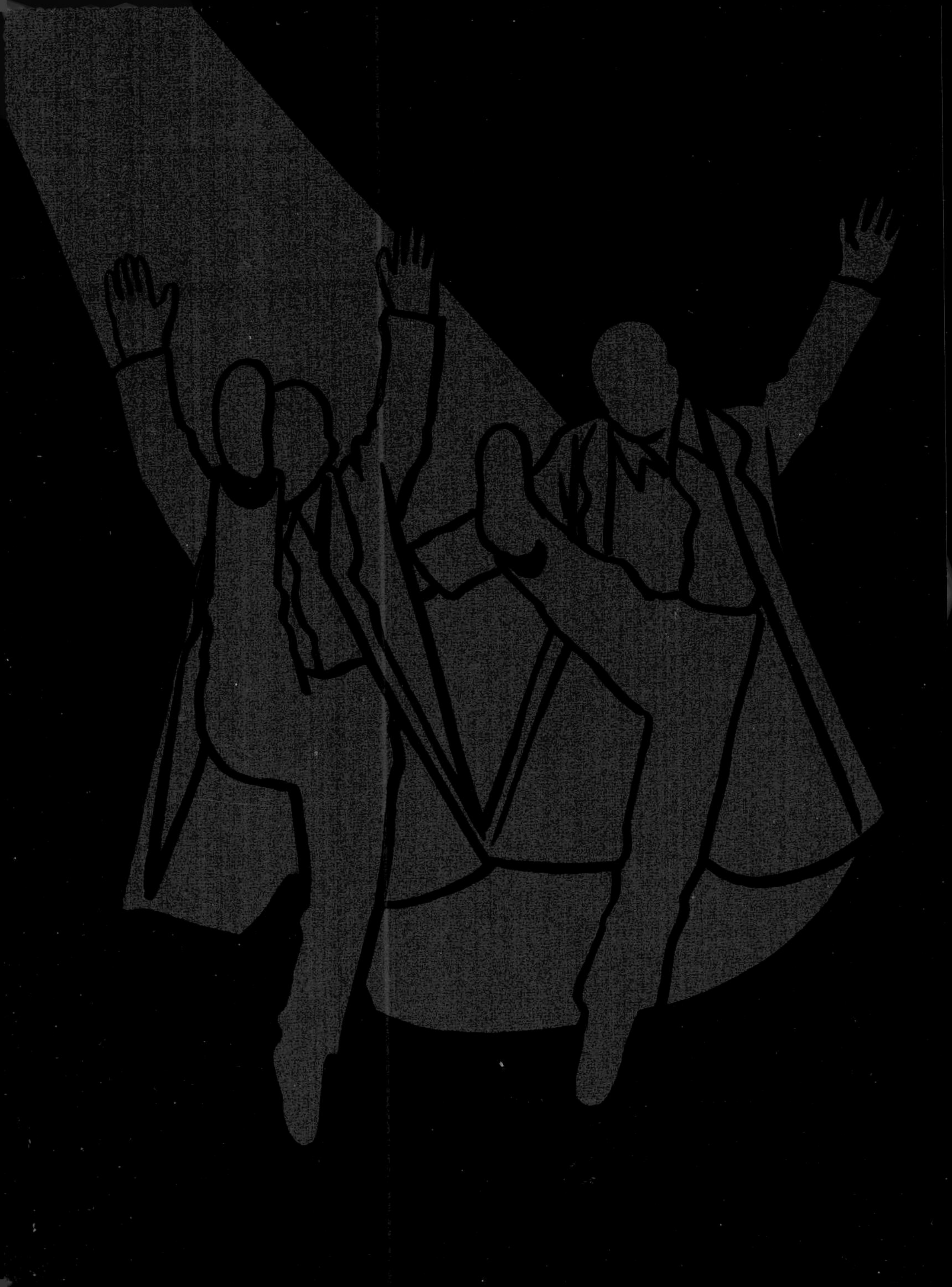

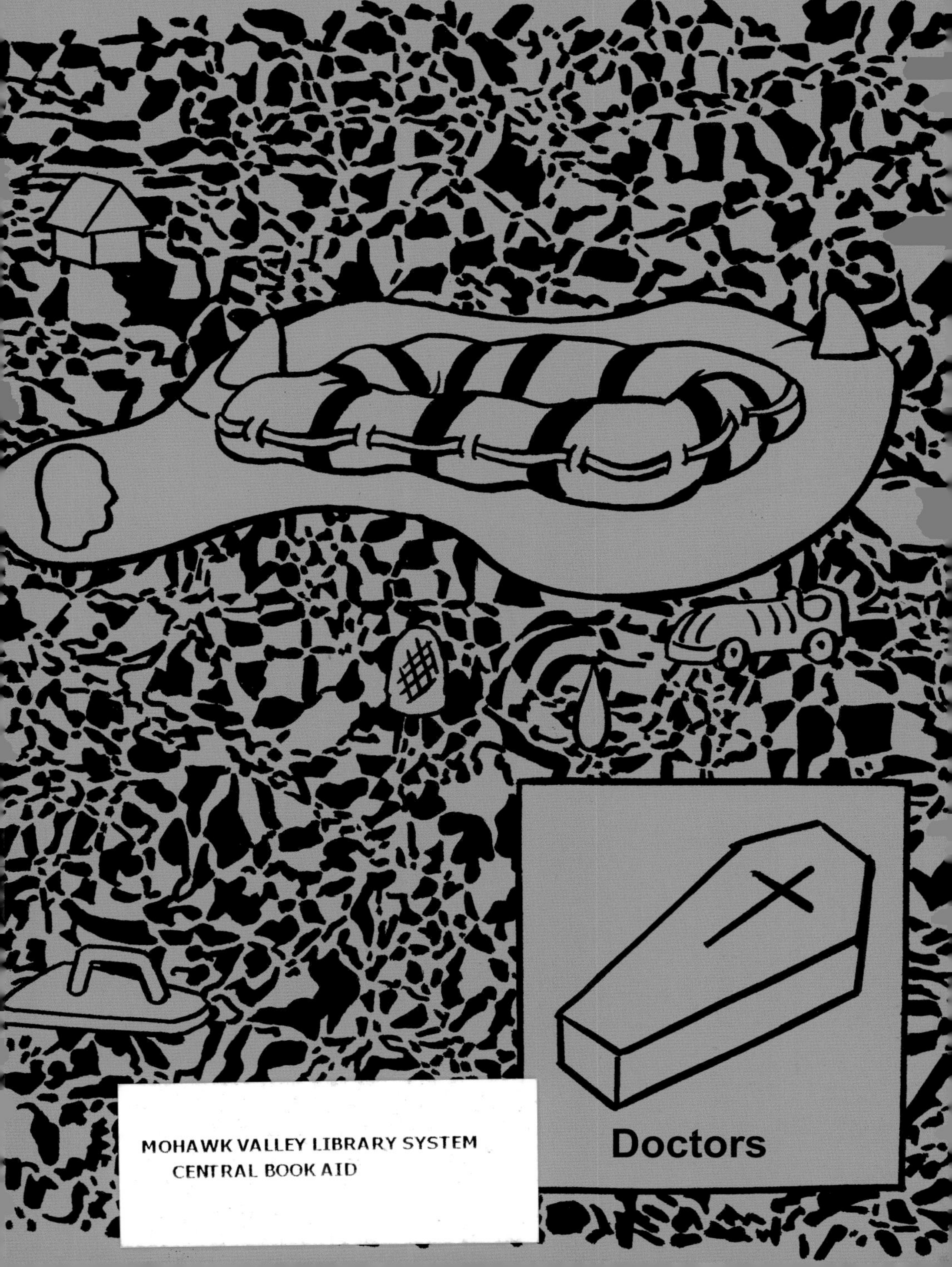
Doctors

Editor and Associate Publisher: Eric Reynolds
Book Design: Dash Shaw
Cover Design: Keeli McCarthy
Production: Paul Baresh
Proofreading: Janice Lee
Publisher: Gary Groth

FANTAGRAPHICS BOOKS, INC.
7563 Lake City Way NE • Seattle, Washington, USA

Doctors is copyright © 2014 Dash Shaw. This edition is copyright © 2014 Fantagraphics Books, Inc. Permission to reproduce content must be obtained from the author or publisher.

ISBN 978-1-60699-803-8

First printing: September, 2014
Printed in Hong Kong

Fantagraphics Books would like thank: Randall Bethune • Big Planet Comics • Black Hook Press, Japan • Nick Capetillo • Kevin Czapiewski • John DiBello • Juan Manuel Domínguez • Mathieu Doublet • Dan Evans III • Thomas Eykemans • Scott Fritsch-Hammes • Coco and Eddie Gorodetsky • Karen Green • Ted Haycraft • Eduardo Takeo "Lizarkeo" Igarashi • Nevdon Jamgochian • Andy Koopmans • Philip Nel • Vanessa Palacios • Kurt Sayenga • Anne Lise Rostgaard Schmidt • Christian Schremser • Secret Headquarters • Paul van Dijken • Mungo van Krimpen-Hall • Jason Aaron Wong • Thomas Zimmermann

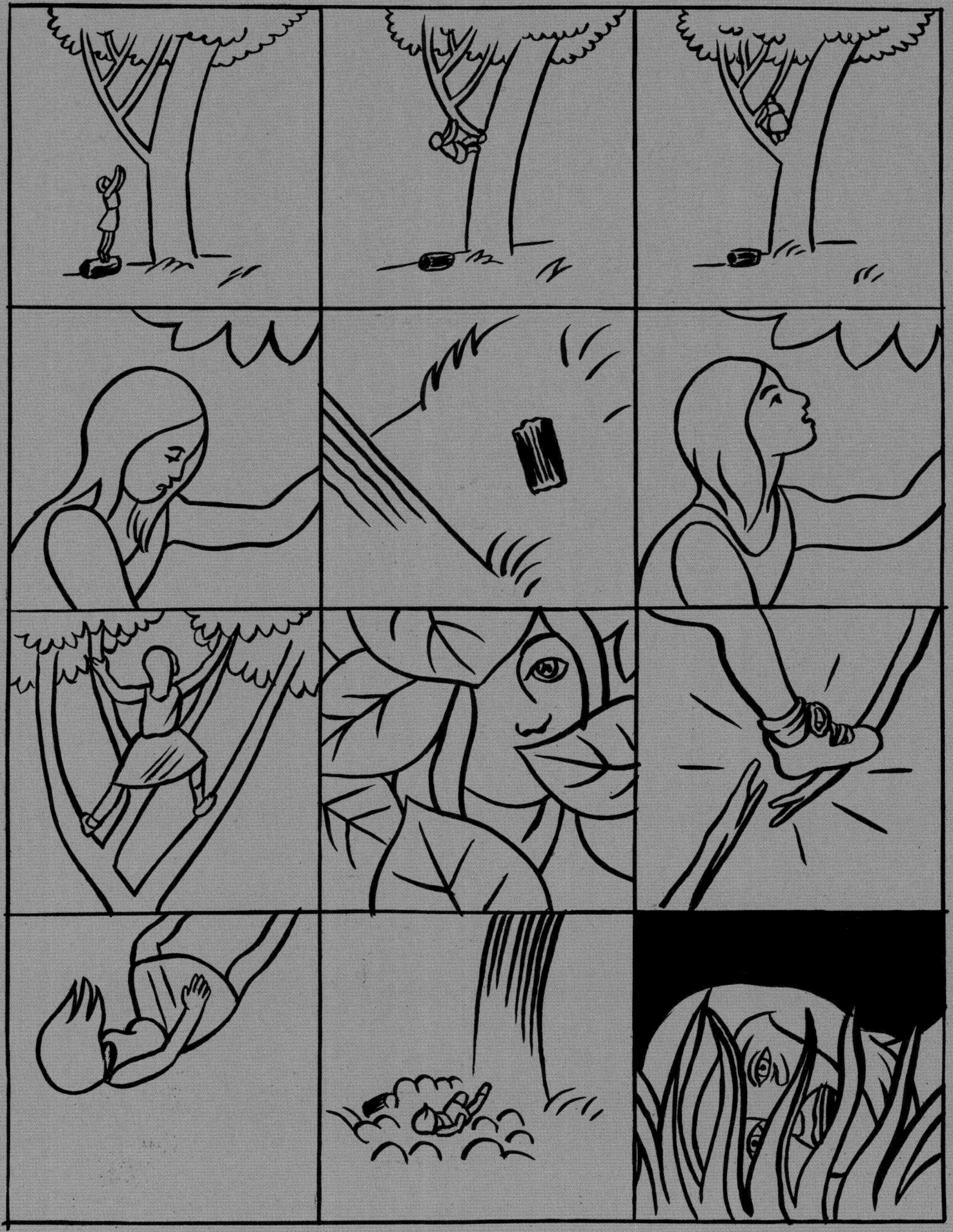

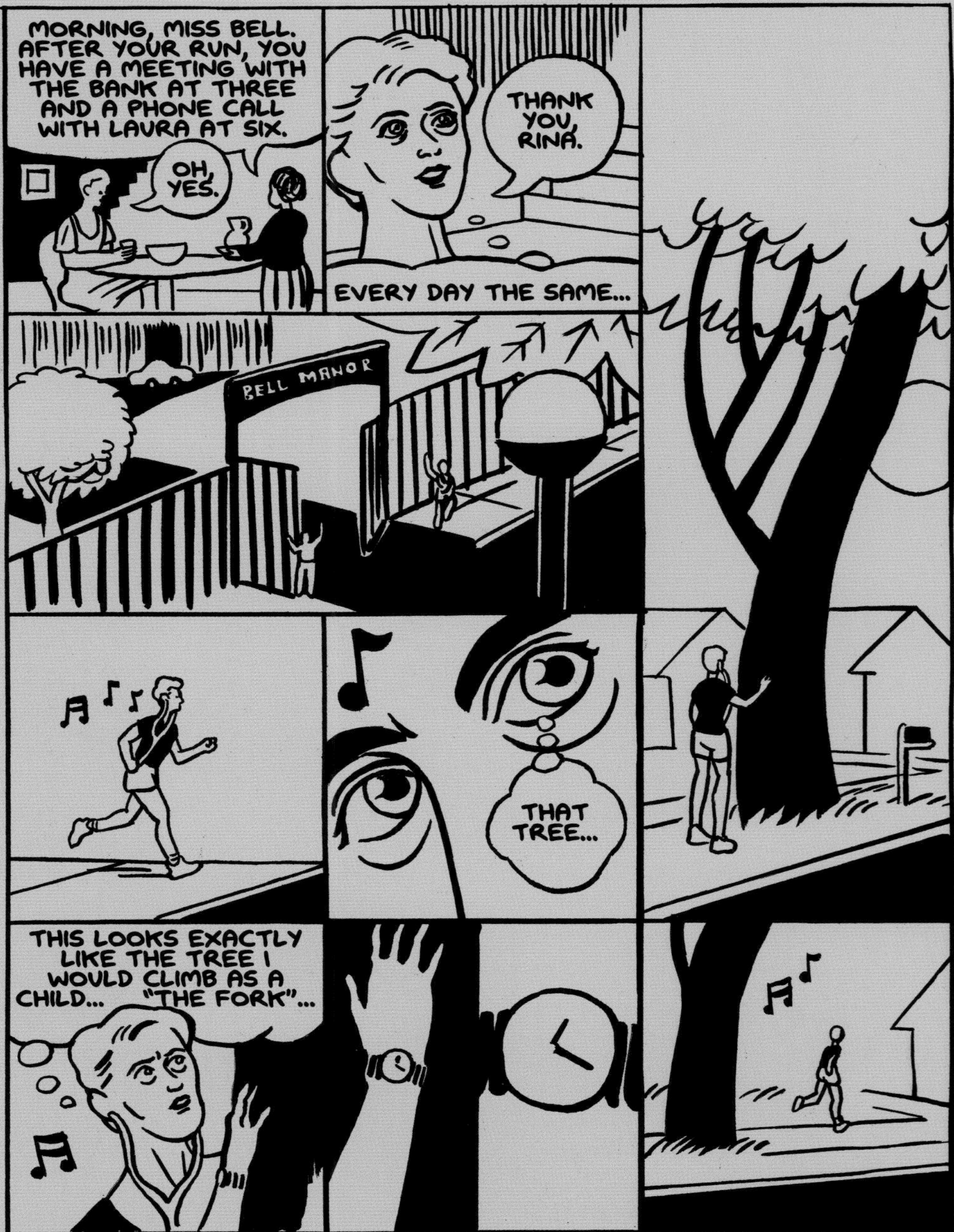
MORNING, MISS BELL. AFTER YOUR RUN, YOU HAVE A MEETING WITH THE BANK AT THREE AND A PHONE CALL WITH LAURA AT SIX.
OH, YES.
THANK YOU, RINA.
EVERY DAY THE SAME...
BELL MANOR
THAT TREE...
THIS LOOKS EXACTLY LIKE THE TREE I WOULD CLIMB AS A CHILD... "THE FORK"...

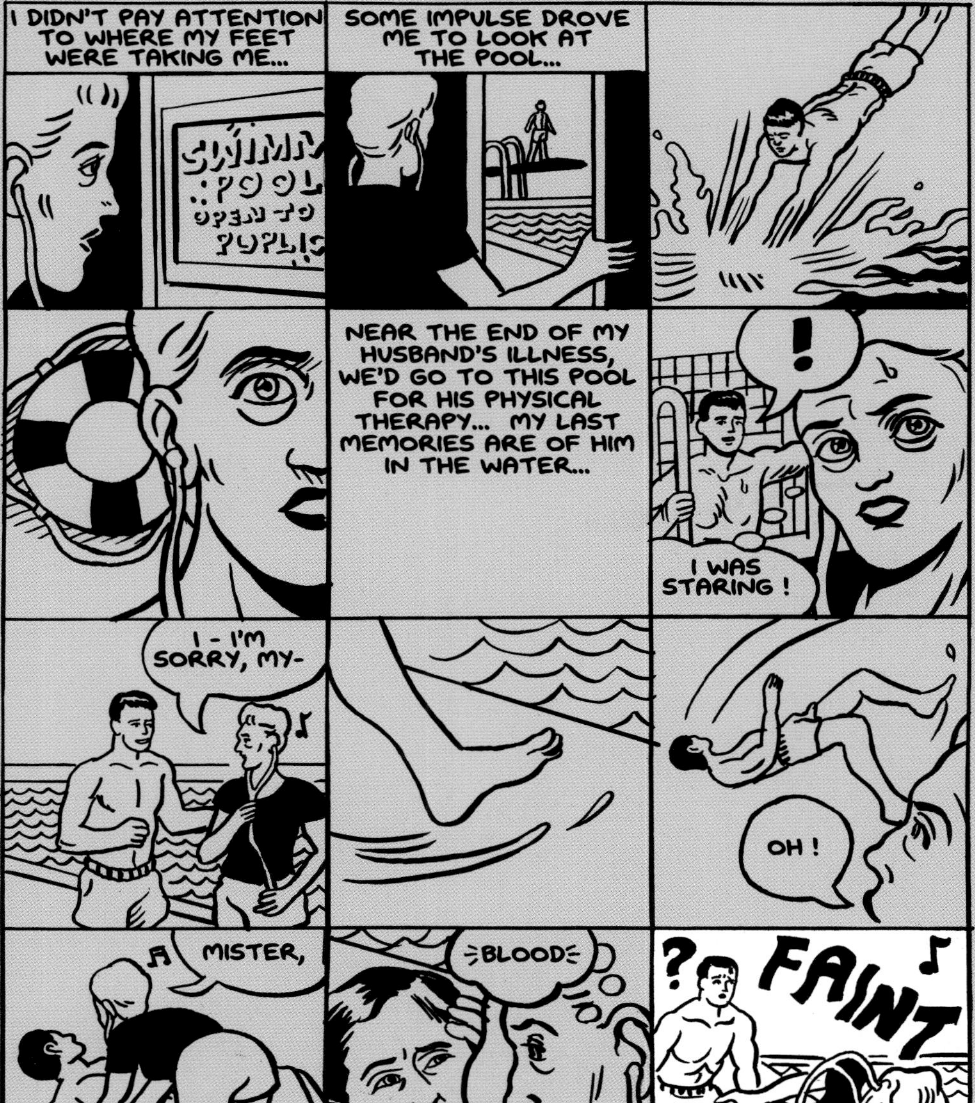
I DIDN'T PAY ATTENTION TO WHERE MY FEET WERE TAKING ME...
SOME IMPULSE DROVE ME TO LOOK AT THE POOL...
NEAR THE END OF MY HUSBAND'S ILLNESS, WE'D GO TO THIS POOL FOR HIS PHYSICAL THERAPY... MY LAST MEMORIES ARE OF HIM IN THE WATER...
!
I WAS STARING !
I - I'M SORRY, MY-
OH !
MISTER,
BLOOD
?
FAINT

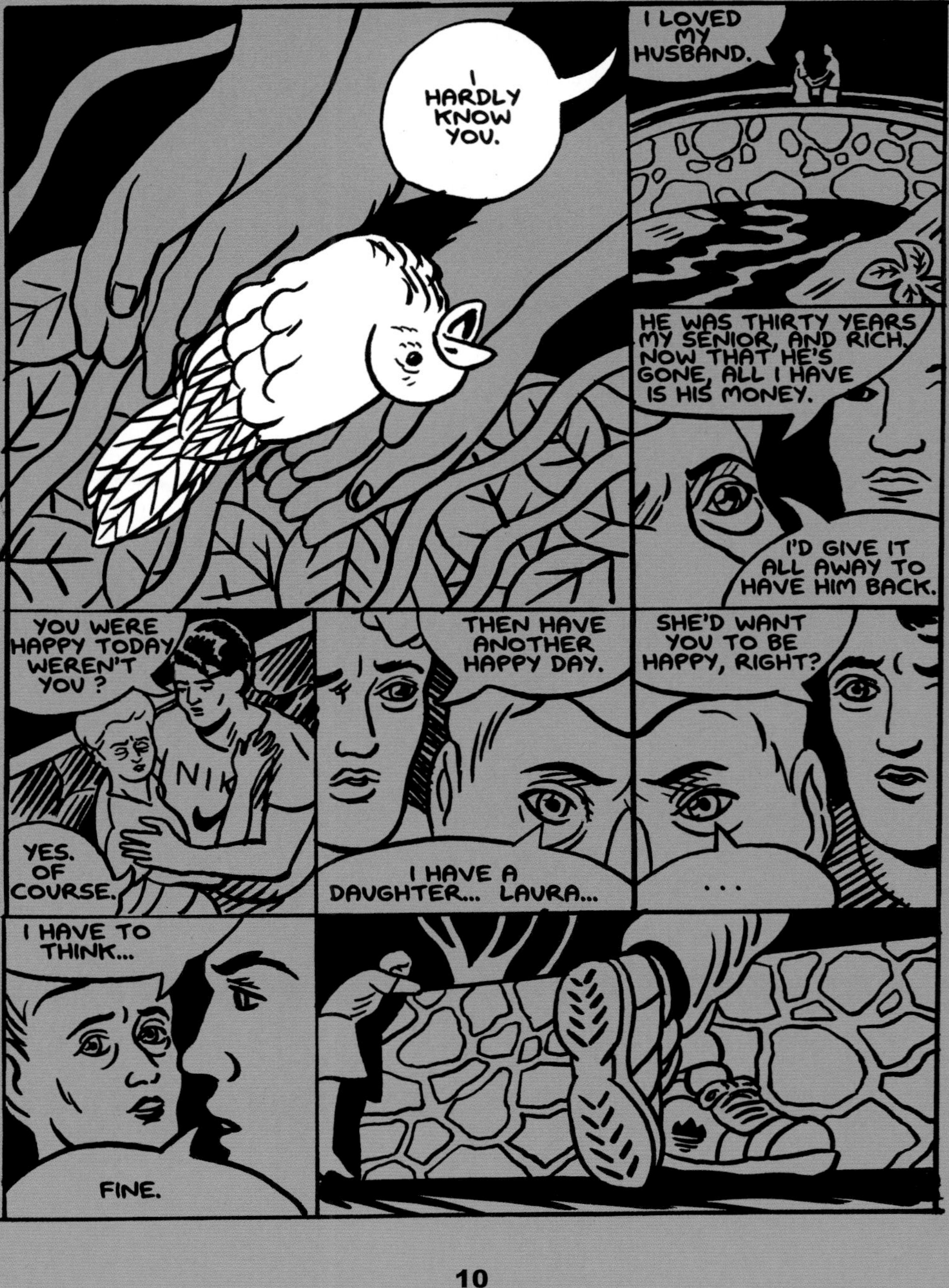

I HARDLY KNOW YOU.
I LOVED MY HUSBAND.
HE WAS THIRTY YEARS MY SENIOR, AND RICH. NOW THAT HE'S GONE, ALL I HAVE IS HIS MONEY.
I'D GIVE IT ALL AWAY TO HAVE HIM BACK.
YOU WERE HAPPY TODAY WEREN'T YOU ?
NIK
YES. OF COURSE.
THEN HAVE ANOTHER HAPPY DAY.
I HAVE A DAUGHTER... LAURA...
SHE'D WANT YOU TO BE HAPPY, RIGHT?
. . .
I HAVE TO THINK...
FINE.

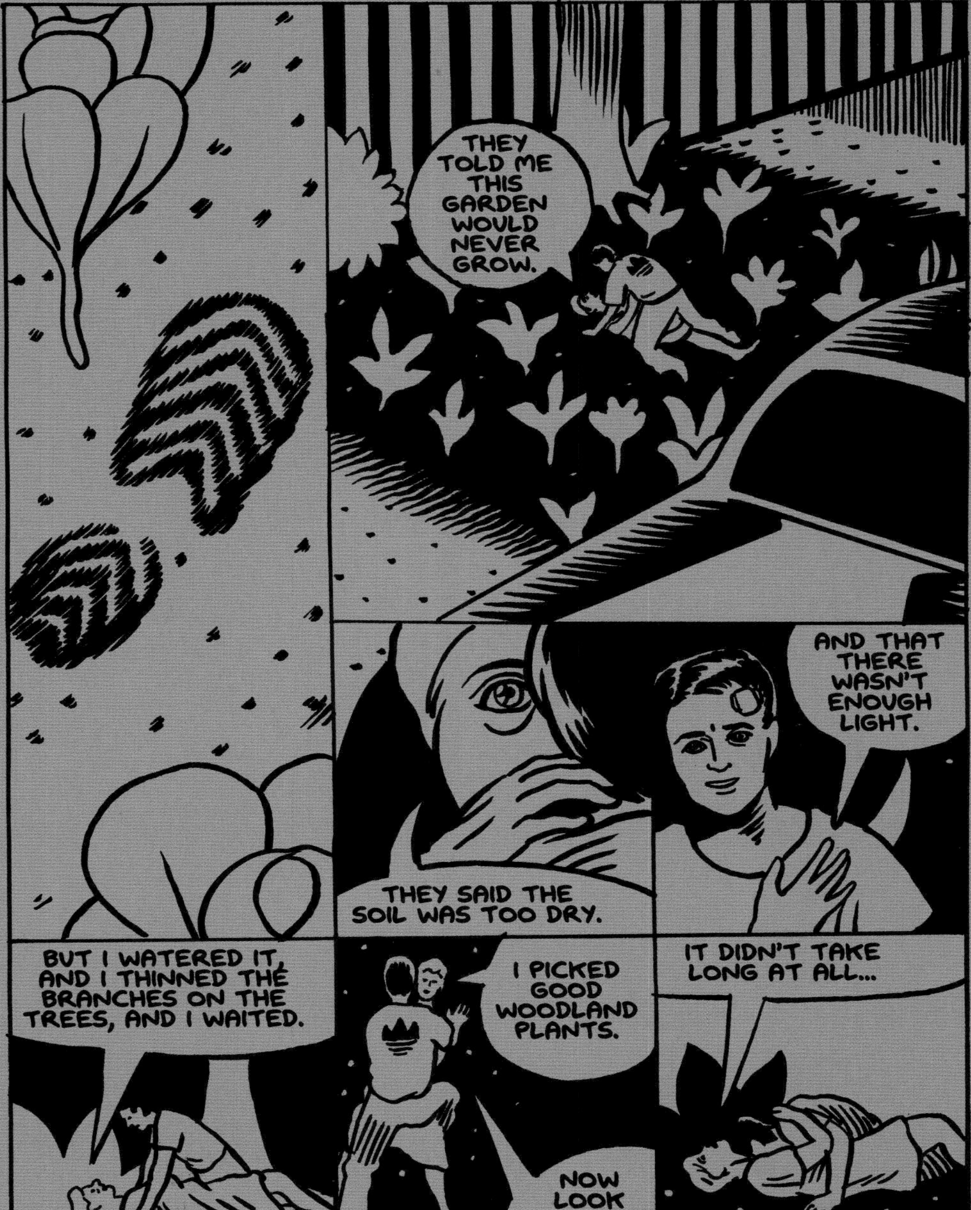

THEY TOLD ME THIS GARDEN WOULD NEVER GROW.
THEY SAID THE SOIL WAS TOO DRY.
AND THAT THERE WASN'T ENOUGH LIGHT.
BUT I WATERED IT, AND I THINNED THE BRANCHES ON THE TREES, AND I WAITED.
I PICKED GOOD WOODLAND PLANTS.
NOW LOOK AT IT...
IT DIDN'T TAKE LONG AT ALL...

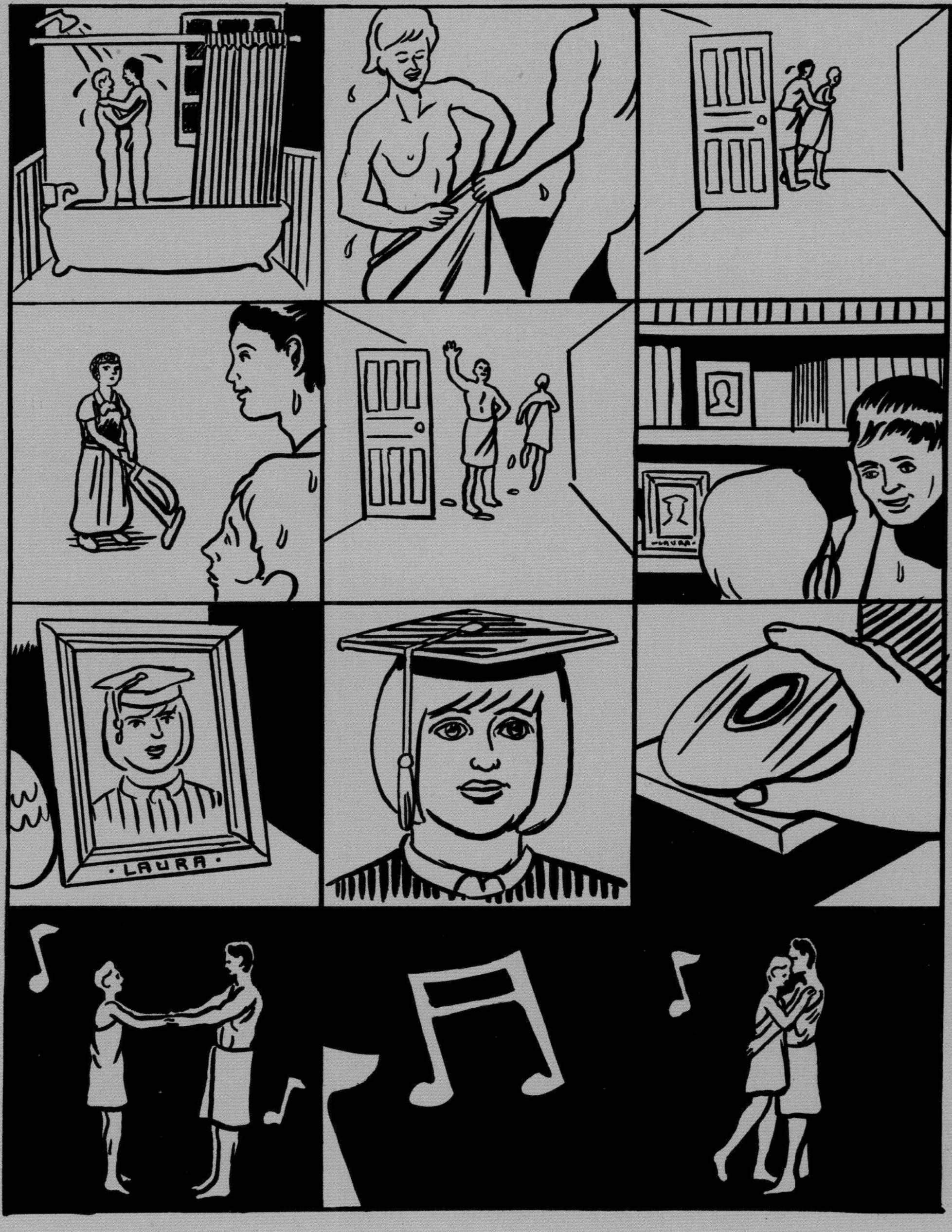
LAURA
LAURA

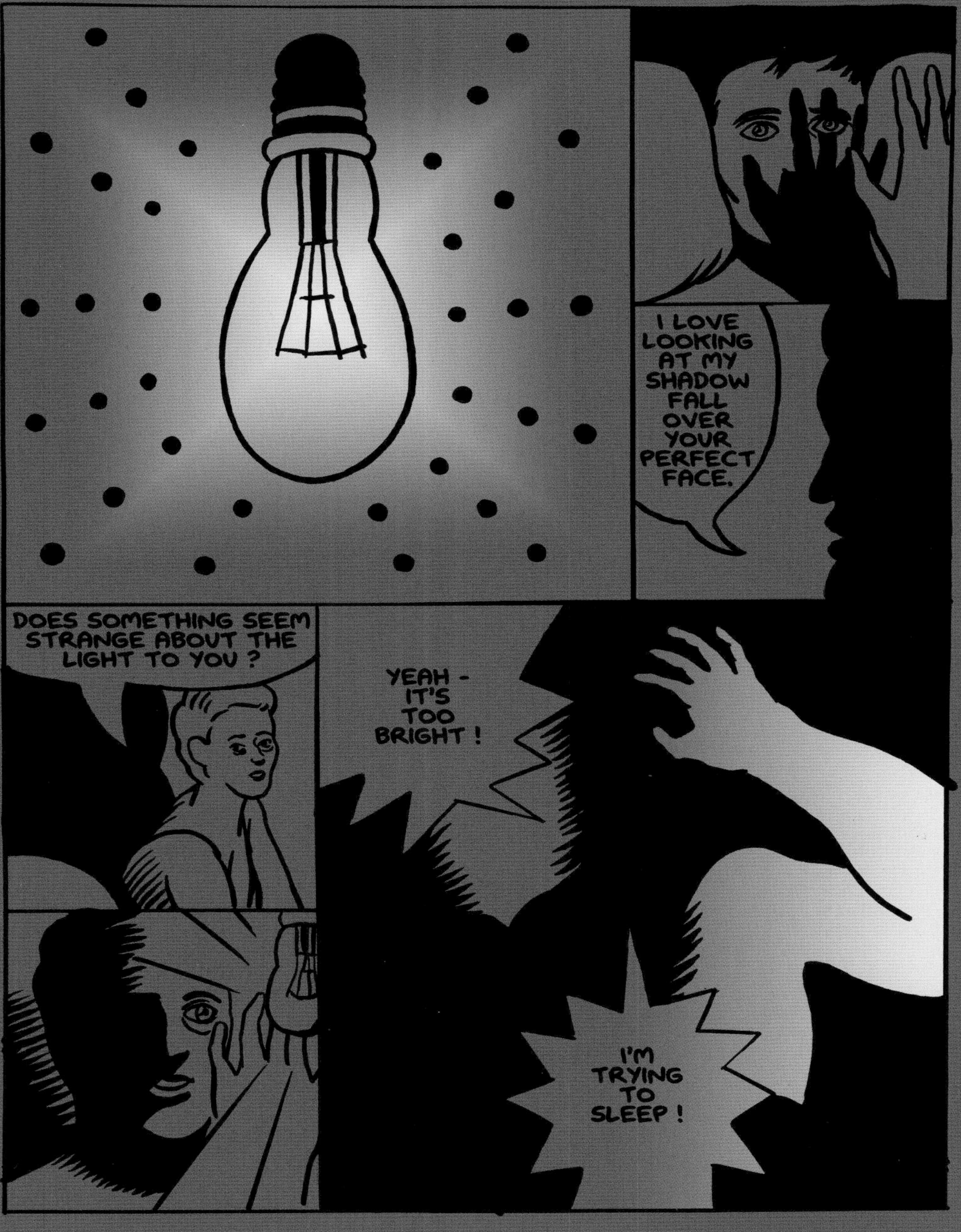
I LOVE LOOKING AT MY SHADOW FALL OVER YOUR PERFECT FACE.
DOES SOMETHING SEEM STRANGE ABOUT THE LIGHT TO YOU ?
YEAH - IT'S TOO BRIGHT !
I'M TRYING TO SLEEP !

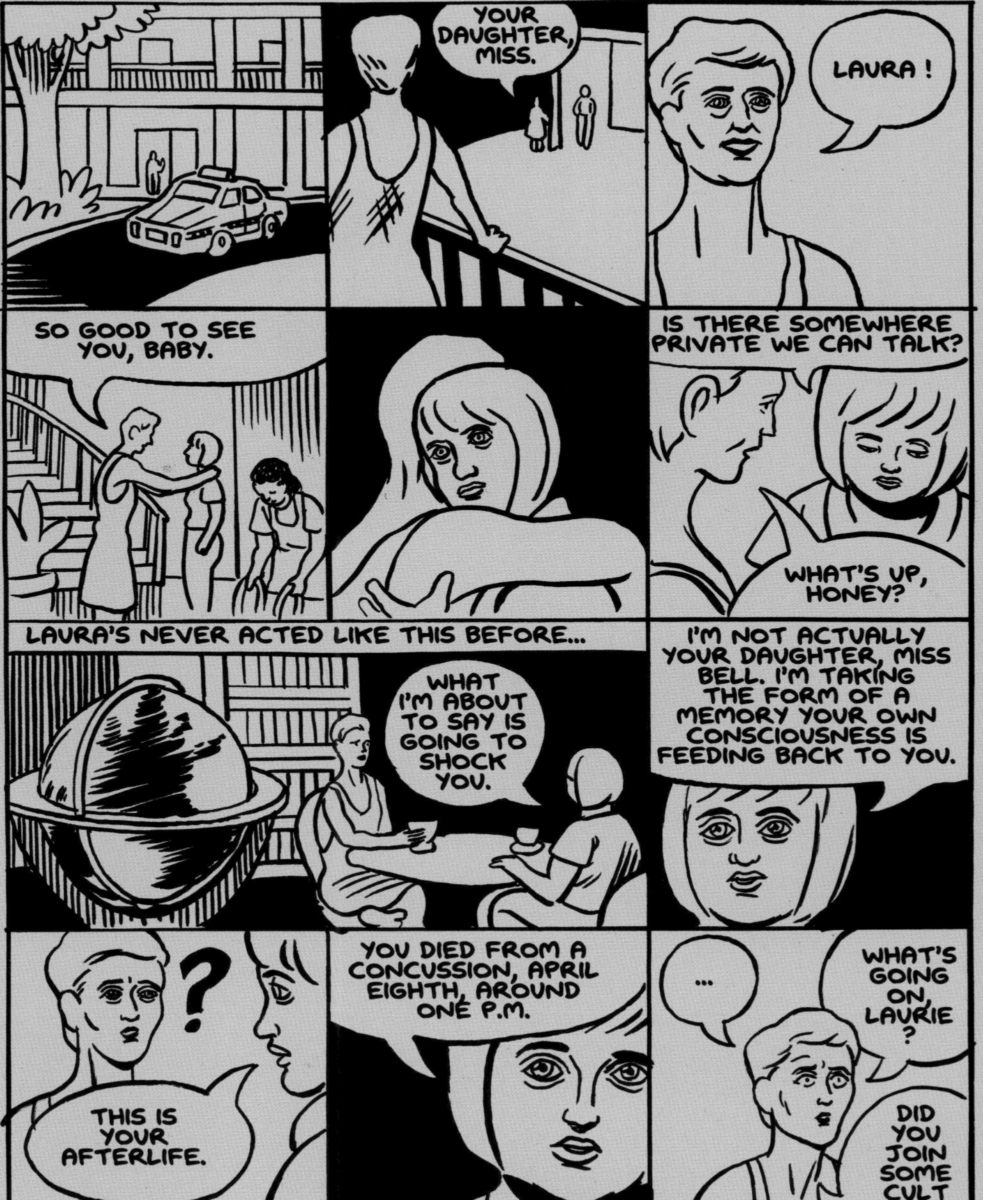
YOUR DAUGHTER, MISS.
LAURA!
SO GOOD TO SEE YOU, BABY.
IS THERE SOMEWHERE PRIVATE WE CAN TALK?
WHAT'S UP, HONEY?
LAURA'S NEVER ACTED LIKE THIS BEFORE...
WHAT I'M ABOUT TO SAY IS GOING TO SHOCK YOU.
I'M NOT ACTUALLY YOUR DAUGHTER, MISS BELL. I'M TAKING THE FORM OF A MEMORY YOUR OWN CONSCIOUSNESS IS FEEDING BACK TO YOU.
?
THIS IS YOUR AFTERLIFE.
YOU DIED FROM A CONCUSSION, APRIL EIGHTH, AROUND ONE P.M.
...
WHAT'S GOING ON, LAURIE?
DID YOU JOIN SOME CULT?

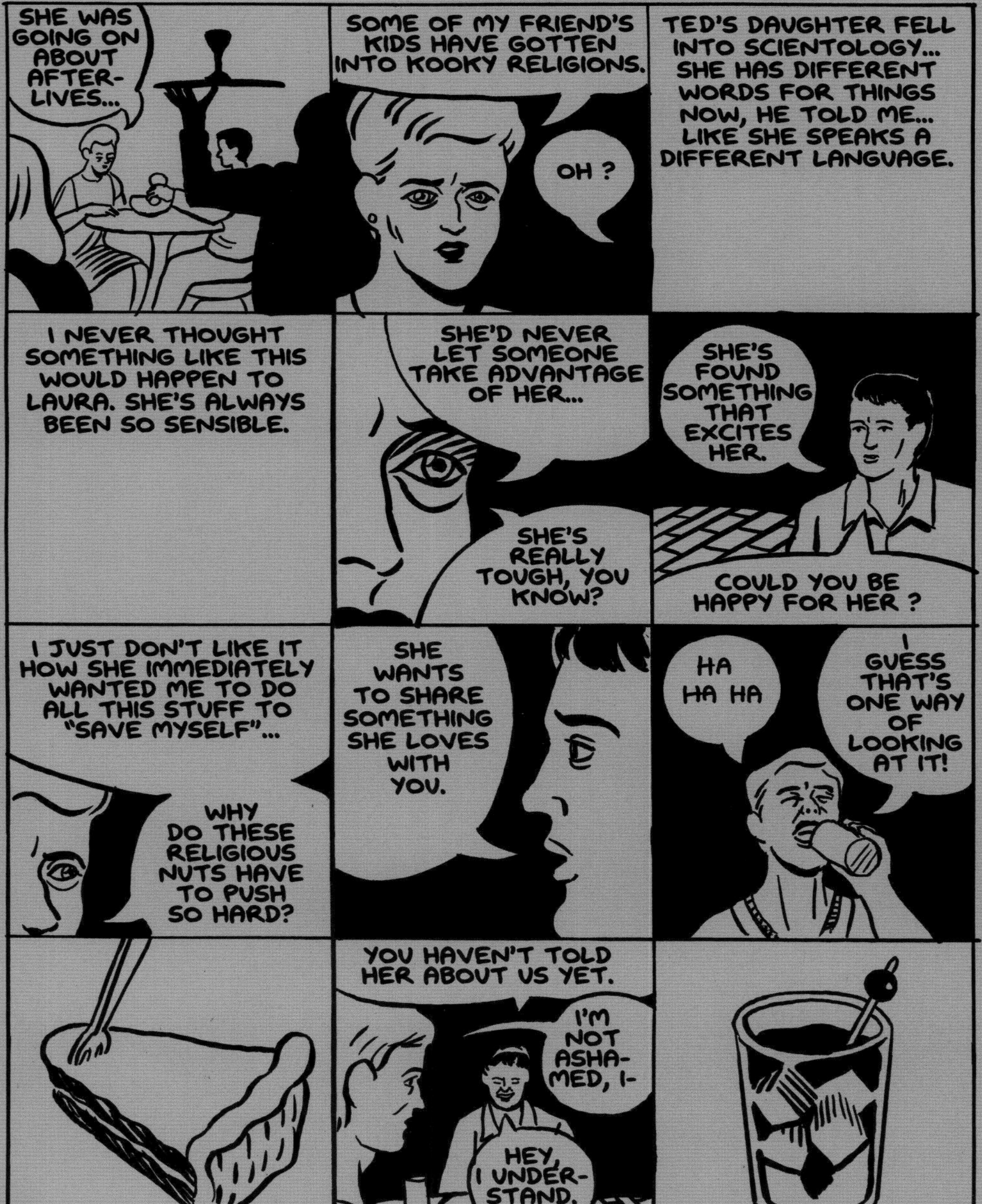

SHE WAS GOING ON ABOUT AFTER-LIVES...
SOME OF MY FRIEND'S KIDS HAVE GOTTEN INTO KOOKY RELIGIONS.
OH ?
TED'S DAUGHTER FELL INTO SCIENTOLOGY... SHE HAS DIFFERENT WORDS FOR THINGS NOW, HE TOLD ME... LIKE SHE SPEAKS A DIFFERENT LANGUAGE.
I NEVER THOUGHT SOMETHING LIKE THIS WOULD HAPPEN TO LAURA. SHE'S ALWAYS BEEN SO SENSIBLE.
SHE'D NEVER LET SOMEONE TAKE ADVANTAGE OF HER...
SHE'S REALLY TOUGH, YOU KNOW?
SHE'S FOUND SOMETHING THAT EXCITES HER.
COULD YOU BE HAPPY FOR HER ?
I JUST DON'T LIKE IT HOW SHE IMMEDIATELY WANTED ME TO DO ALL THIS STUFF TO "SAVE MYSELF"...
WHY DO THESE RELIGIOUS NUTS HAVE TO PUSH SO HARD?
SHE WANTS TO SHARE SOMETHING SHE LOVES WITH YOU.
HA HA HA
I GUESS THAT'S ONE WAY OF LOOKING AT IT!
YOU HAVEN'T TOLD HER ABOUT US YET.
I'M NOT ASHA-MED, I-
HEY, I UNDER-STAND.

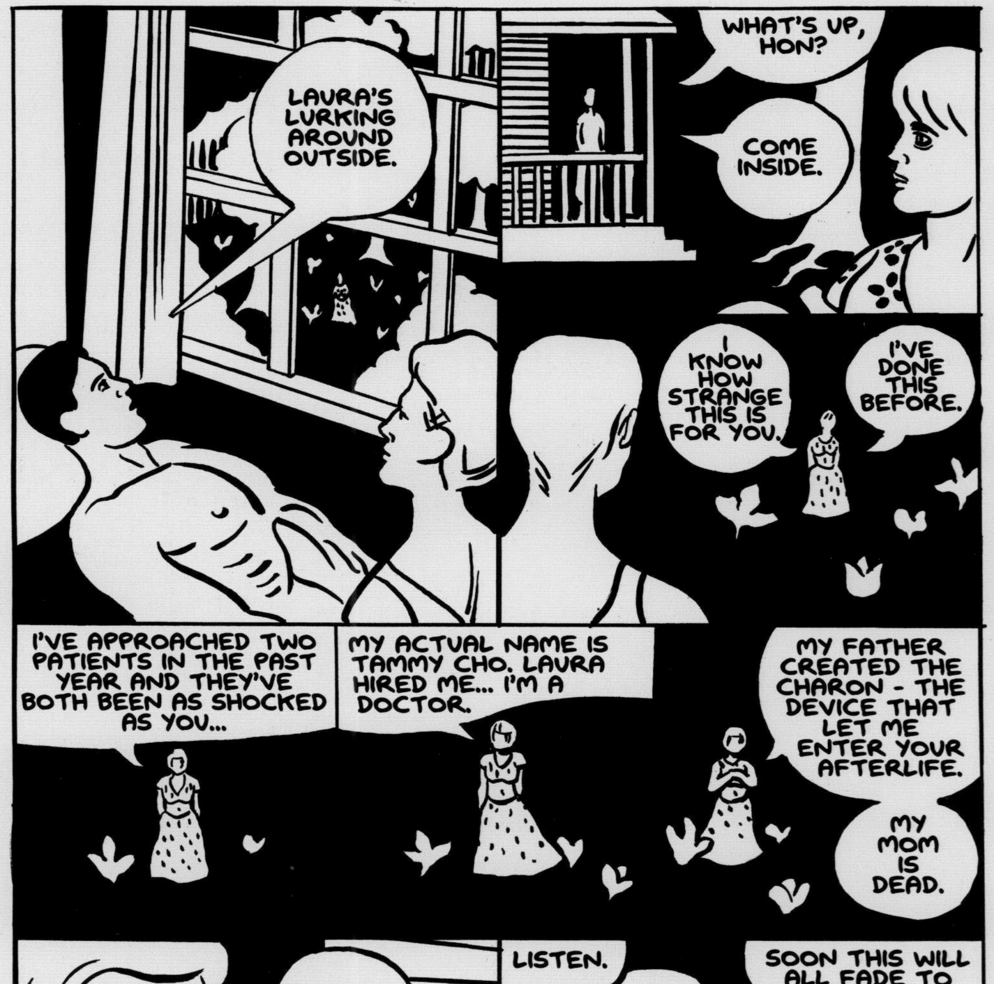
LAURA'S LURKING AROUND OUTSIDE.
WHAT'S UP, HON?
COME INSIDE.
I KNOW HOW STRANGE THIS IS FOR YOU.
I'VE DONE THIS BEFORE.
I'VE APPROACHED TWO PATIENTS IN THE PAST YEAR AND THEY'VE BOTH BEEN AS SHOCKED AS YOU...
MY ACTUAL NAME IS TAMMY CHO. LAURA HIRED ME... I'M A DOCTOR.
MY FATHER CREATED THE CHARON - THE DEVICE THAT LET ME ENTER YOUR AFTERLIFE.
MY MOM IS DEAD.
BABY.
YOU'RE BREAKING MY HEART.
LISTEN.
SOON THIS WILL ALL FADE TO BLACK...
HELP ME HELP YOU COME BACK TO LIFE.

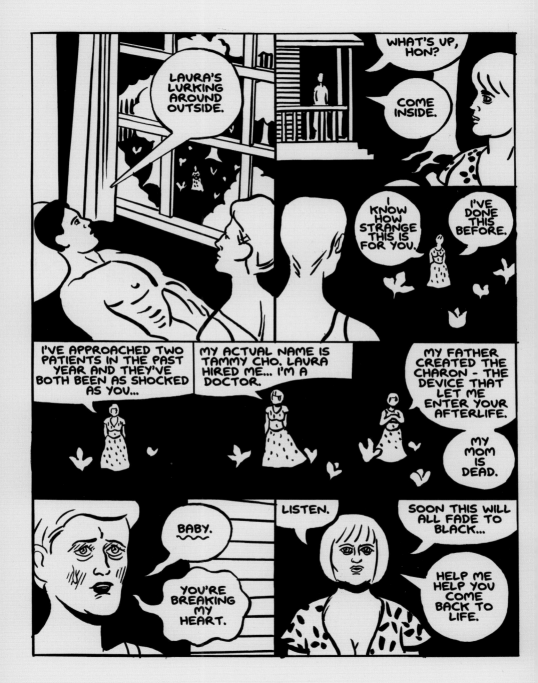

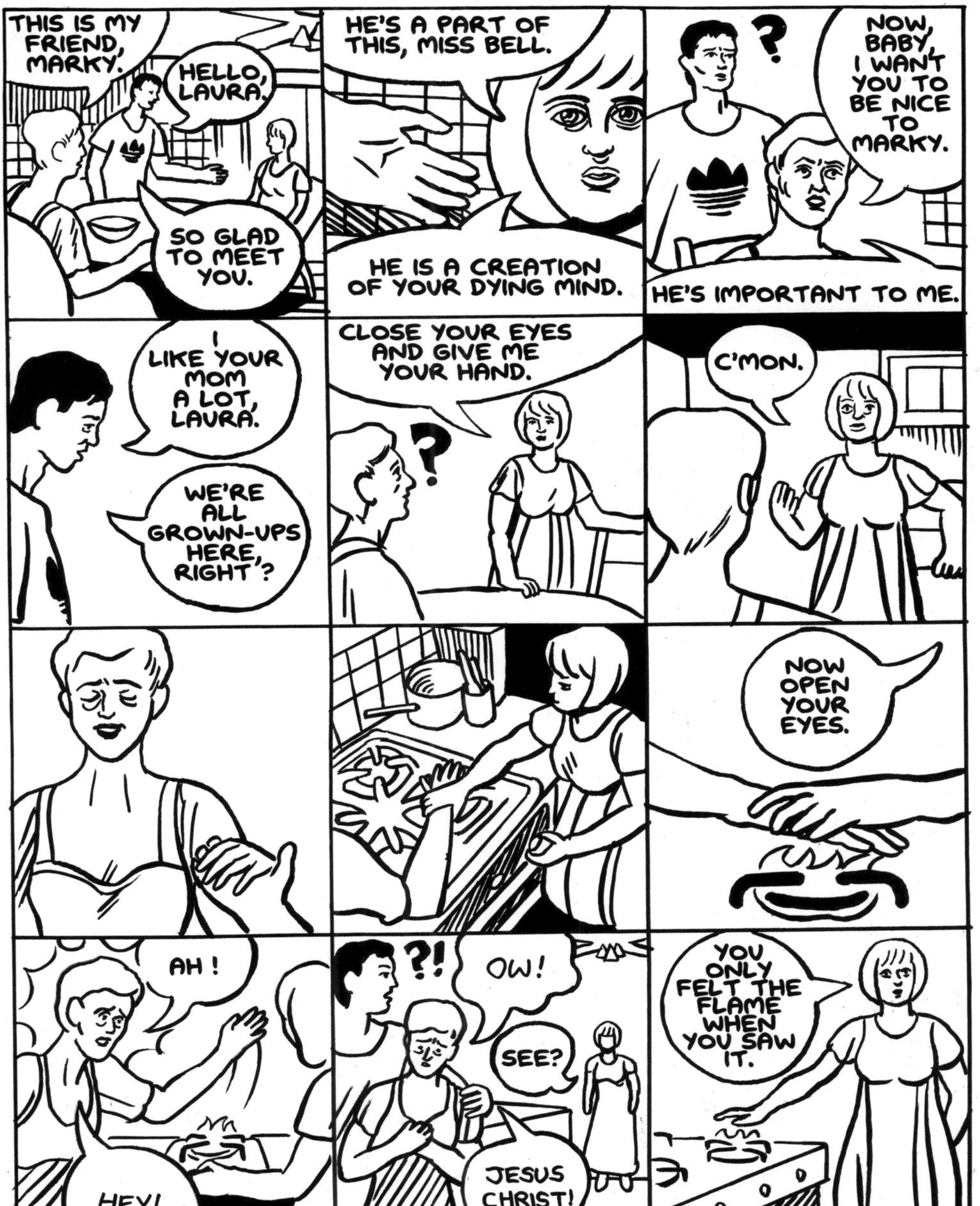
THIS IS MY FRIEND, MARKY.
HELLO, LAURA.
SO GLAD TO MEET YOU.
HE'S A PART OF THIS, MISS BELL.
HE IS A CREATION OF YOUR DYING MIND.
?
NOW, BABY, I WANT YOU TO BE NICE TO MARKY.
HE'S IMPORTANT TO ME.
I LIKE YOUR MOM A LOT, LAURA.
WE'RE ALL GROWN-UPS HERE, RIGHT?
CLOSE YOUR EYES AND GIVE ME YOUR HAND.
?
C'MON.
NOW OPEN YOUR EYES.
AH!
HEY!
?!
OW!
SEE?
JESUS CHRIST!
YOU ONLY FELT THE FLAME WHEN YOU SAW IT.

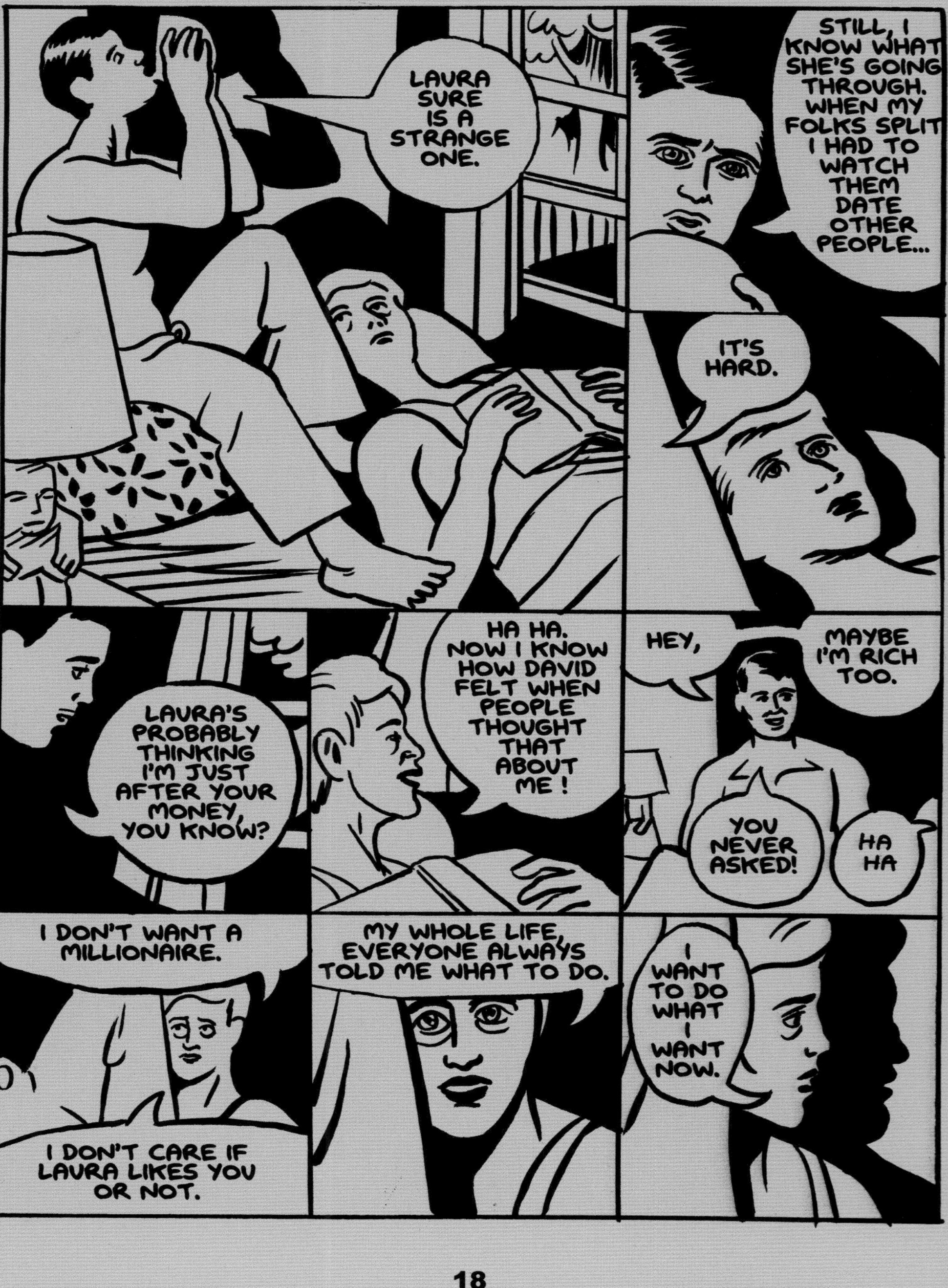
LAURA SURE IS A STRANGE ONE.
STILL, I KNOW WHAT SHE'S GOING THROUGH. WHEN MY FOLKS SPLIT I HAD TO WATCH THEM DATE OTHER PEOPLE...
IT'S HARD.
LAURA'S PROBABLY THINKING I'M JUST AFTER YOUR MONEY, YOU KNOW?
HA HA. NOW I KNOW HOW DAVID FELT WHEN PEOPLE THOUGHT THAT ABOUT ME!
HEY,
MAYBE I'M RICH TOO.
YOU NEVER ASKED!
HA HA
I DON'T WANT A MILLIONAIRE.
I DON'T CARE IF LAURA LIKES YOU OR NOT.
MY WHOLE LIFE, EVERYONE ALWAYS TOLD ME WHAT TO DO.
I WANT TO DO WHAT I WANT NOW.

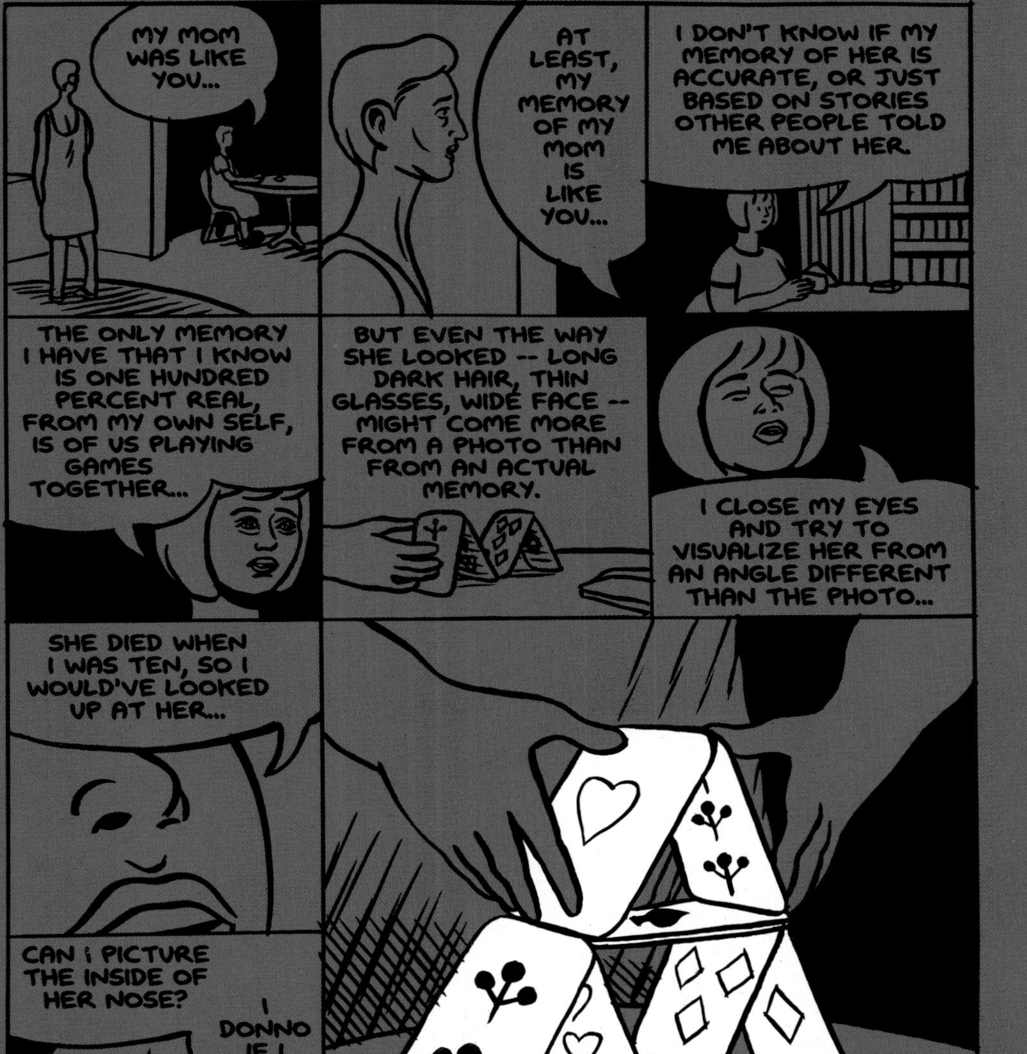
MY MOM WAS LIKE YOU...
AT LEAST, MY MEMORY OF MY MOM IS LIKE YOU...
I DON'T KNOW IF MY MEMORY OF HER IS ACCURATE, OR JUST BASED ON STORIES OTHER PEOPLE TOLD ME ABOUT HER.
THE ONLY MEMORY I HAVE THAT I KNOW IS ONE HUNDRED PERCENT REAL, FROM MY OWN SELF, IS OF US PLAYING GAMES TOGETHER...
BUT EVEN THE WAY SHE LOOKED -- LONG DARK HAIR, THIN GLASSES, WIDE FACE -- MIGHT COME MORE FROM A PHOTO THAN FROM AN ACTUAL MEMORY.
I CLOSE MY EYES AND TRY TO VISUALIZE HER FROM AN ANGLE DIFFERENT THAN THE PHOTO...
SHE DIED WHEN I WAS TEN, SO I WOULD'VE LOOKED UP AT HER...
CAN I PICTURE THE INSIDE OF HER NOSE?
I DONNO IF I CAN...
HA HA.

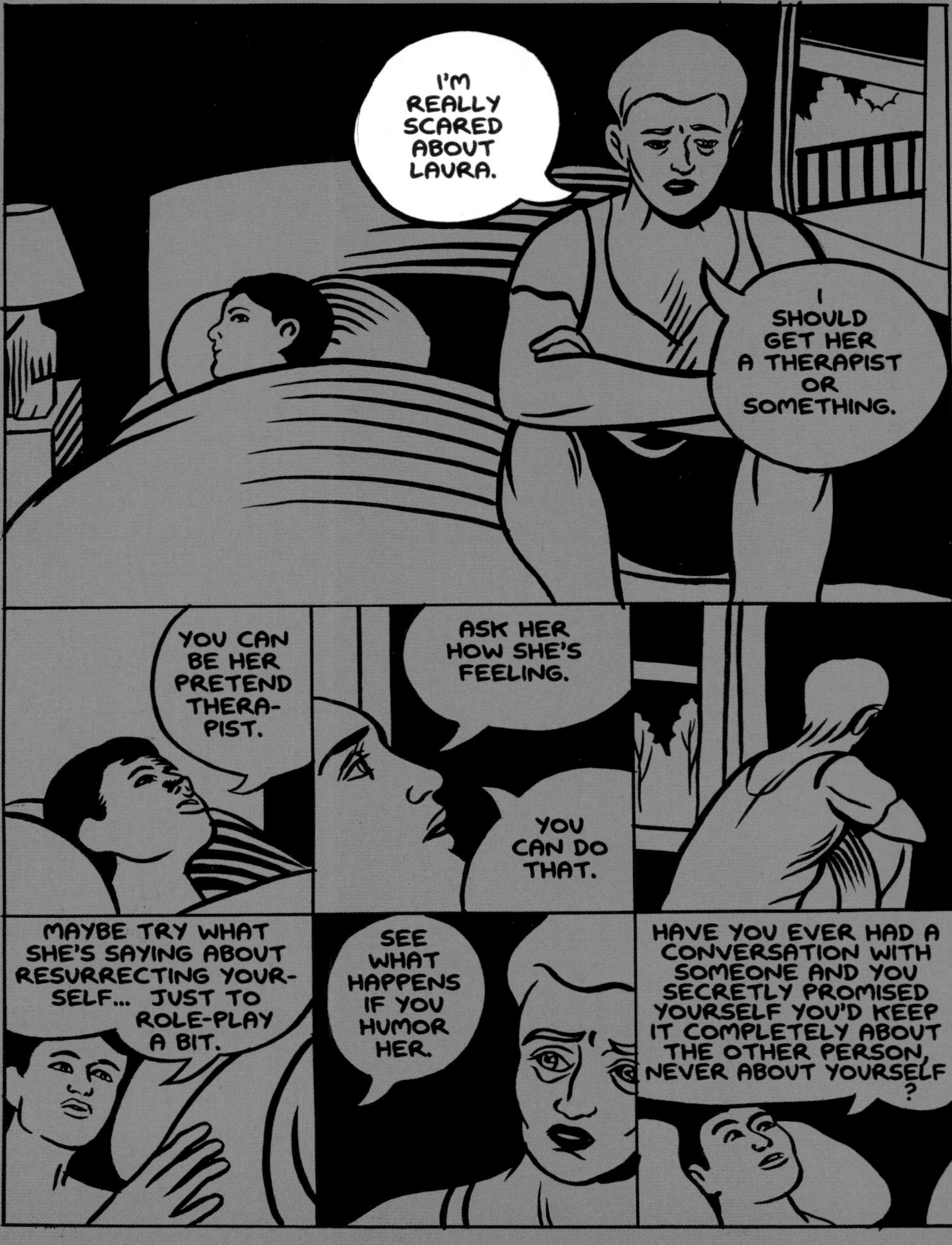
I'M REALLY SCARED ABOUT LAURA.
I SHOULD GET HER A THERAPIST OR SOMETHING.
YOU CAN BE HER PRETEND THERA-PIST.
ASK HER HOW SHE'S FEELING.
YOU CAN DO THAT.
MAYBE TRY WHAT SHE'S SAYING ABOUT RESURRECTING YOUR-SELF... JUST TO ROLE-PLAY A BIT.
SEE WHAT HAPPENS IF YOU HUMOR HER.
HAVE YOU EVER HAD A CONVERSATION WITH SOMEONE AND YOU SECRETLY PROMISED YOURSELF YOU'D KEEP IT COMPLETELY ABOUT THE OTHER PERSON, NEVER ABOUT YOURSELF?

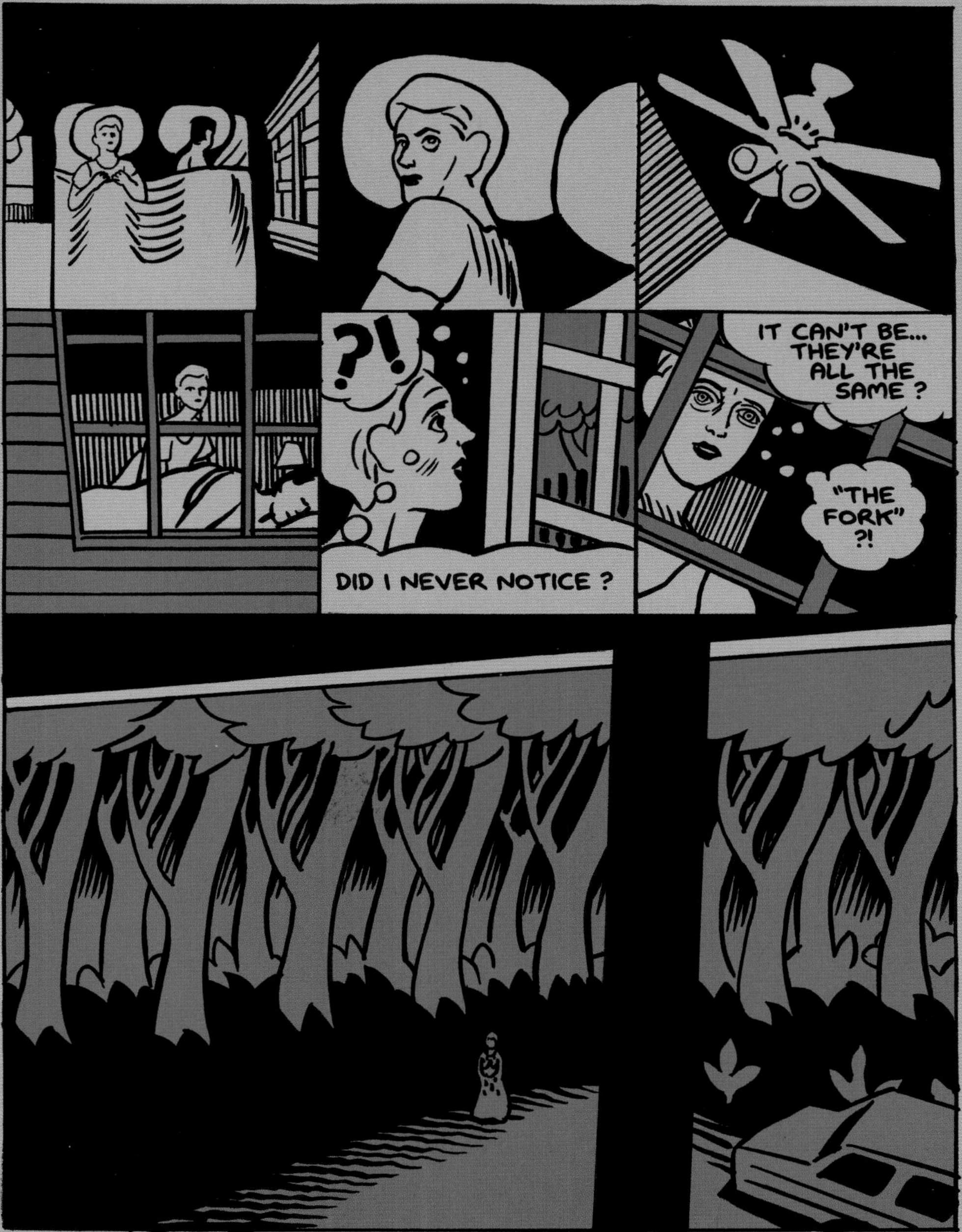
?!
DID I NEVER NOTICE ?
IT CAN'T BE... THEY'RE ALL THE SAME ?
"THE FORK" ?!

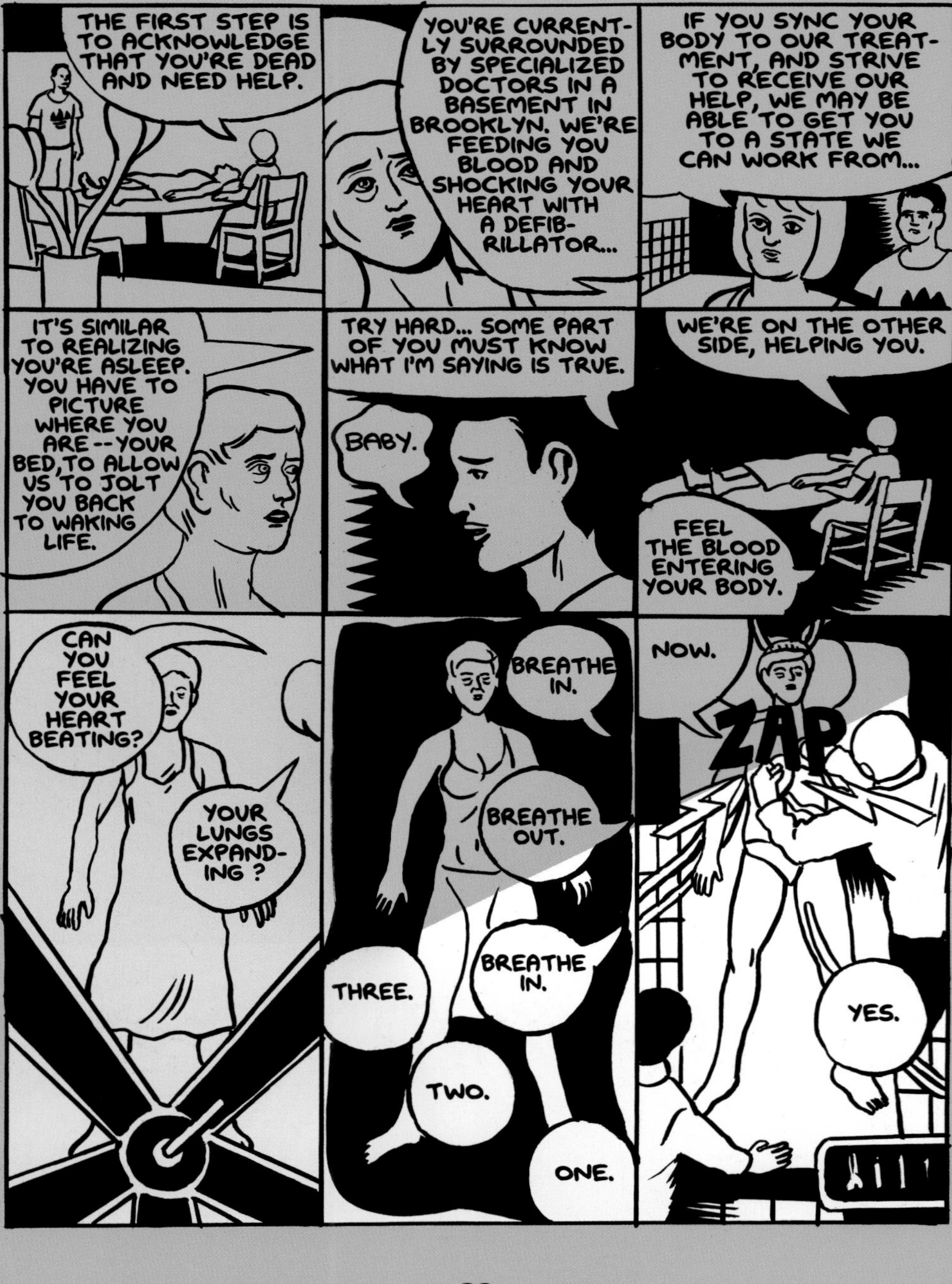

THE FIRST STEP IS TO ACKNOWLEDGE THAT YOU'RE DEAD AND NEED HELP.
YOU'RE CURRENTLY SURROUNDED BY SPECIALIZED DOCTORS IN A BASEMENT IN BROOKLYN. WE'RE FEEDING YOU BLOOD AND SHOCKING YOUR HEART WITH A DEFIBRILLATOR...
IF YOU SYNC YOUR BODY TO OUR TREATMENT, AND STRIVE TO RECEIVE OUR HELP, WE MAY BE ABLE TO GET YOU TO A STATE WE CAN WORK FROM...
IT'S SIMILAR TO REALIZING YOU'RE ASLEEP. YOU HAVE TO PICTURE WHERE YOU ARE--YOUR BED, TO ALLOW US TO JOLT YOU BACK TO WAKING LIFE.
TRY HARD... SOME PART OF YOU MUST KNOW WHAT I'M SAYING IS TRUE.
BABY.
WE'RE ON THE OTHER SIDE, HELPING YOU.
FEEL THE BLOOD ENTERING YOUR BODY.
CAN YOU FEEL YOUR HEART BEATING?
YOUR LUNGS EXPANDING?
BREATHE IN.
BREATHE OUT.
THREE.
BREATHE IN.
TWO.
ONE.
NOW.
ZAP
YES.

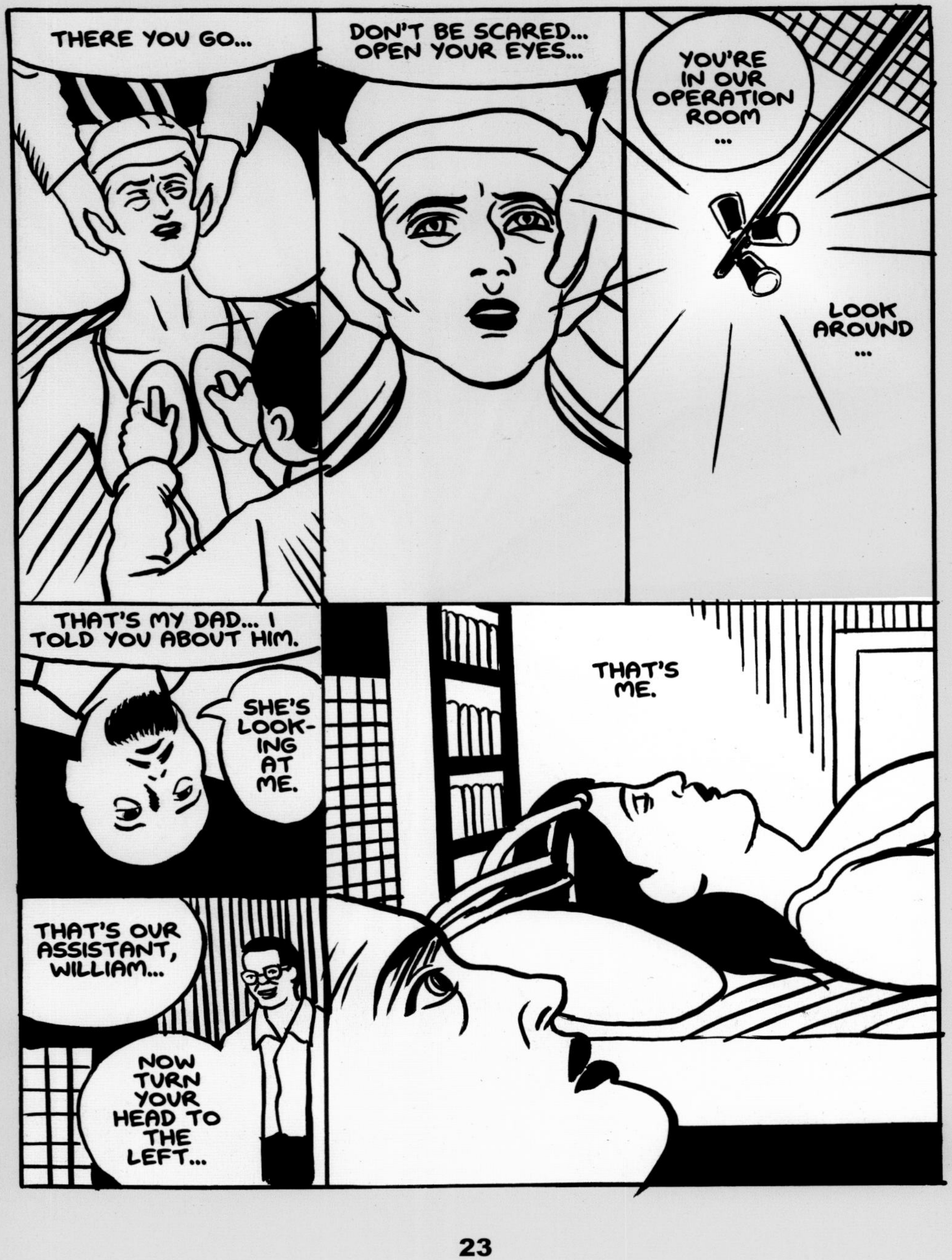
THERE YOU GO...
DON'T BE SCARED... OPEN YOUR EYES...
YOU'RE IN OUR OPERATION ROOM ...
LOOK AROUND ...
THAT'S MY DAD... I TOLD YOU ABOUT HIM.
SHE'S LOOK-ING AT ME.
THAT'S ME.
THAT'S OUR ASSISTANT, WILLIAM...
NOW TURN YOUR HEAD TO THE LEFT...

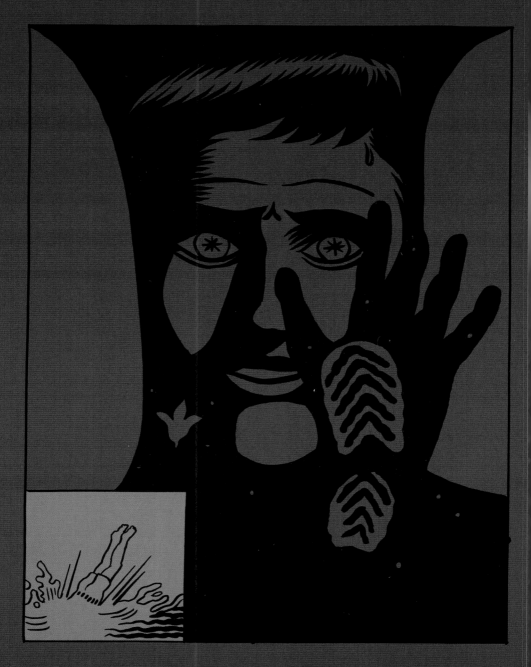

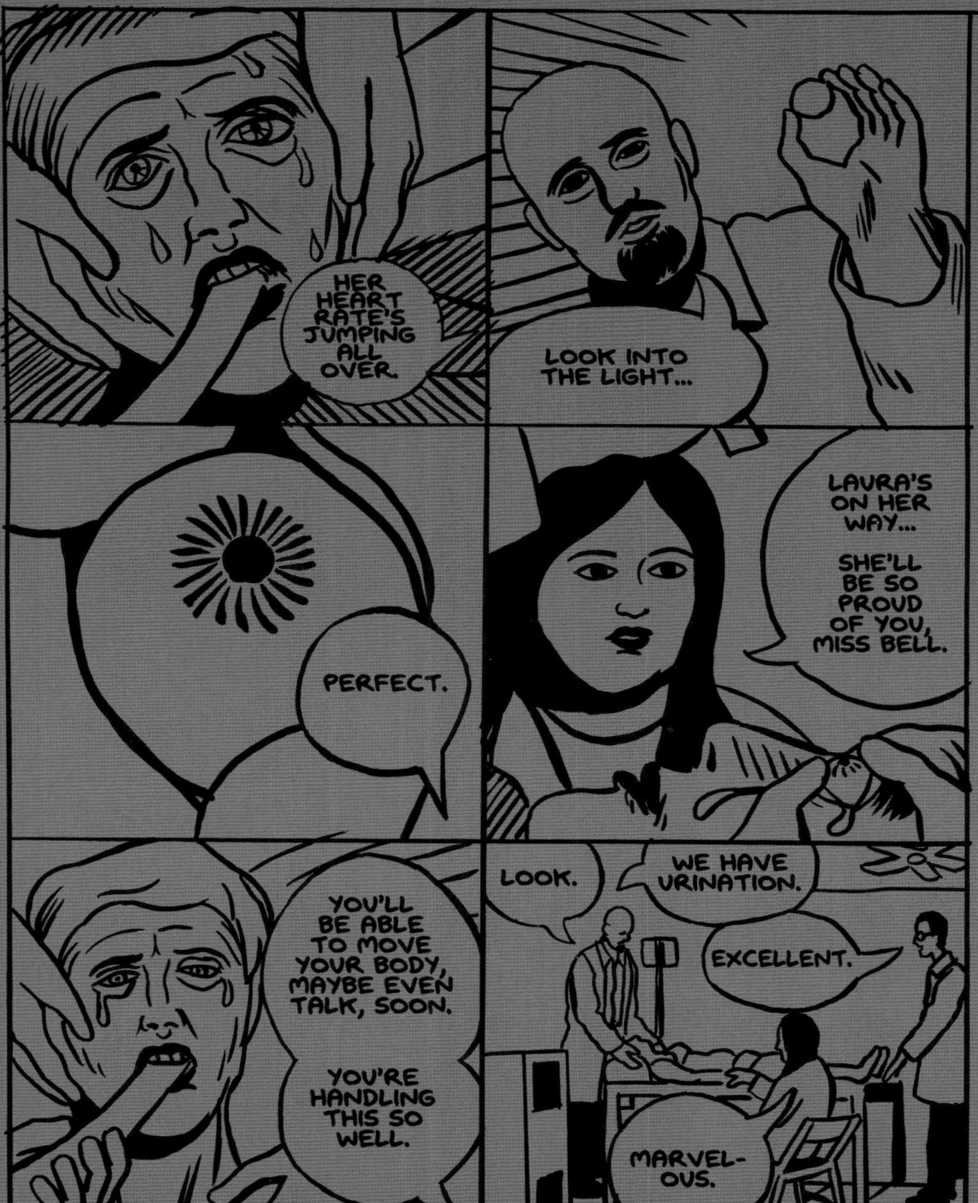
HER HEART RATE'S JUMPING ALL OVER.
LOOK INTO THE LIGHT...
PERFECT.
LAURA'S ON HER WAY...
SHE'LL BE SO PROUD OF YOU, MISS BELL.
YOU'LL BE ABLE TO MOVE YOUR BODY, MAYBE EVEN TALK, SOON.
YOU'RE HANDLING THIS SO WELL.
LOOK.
WE HAVE URINATION.
EXCELLENT.
MARVEL-OUS.

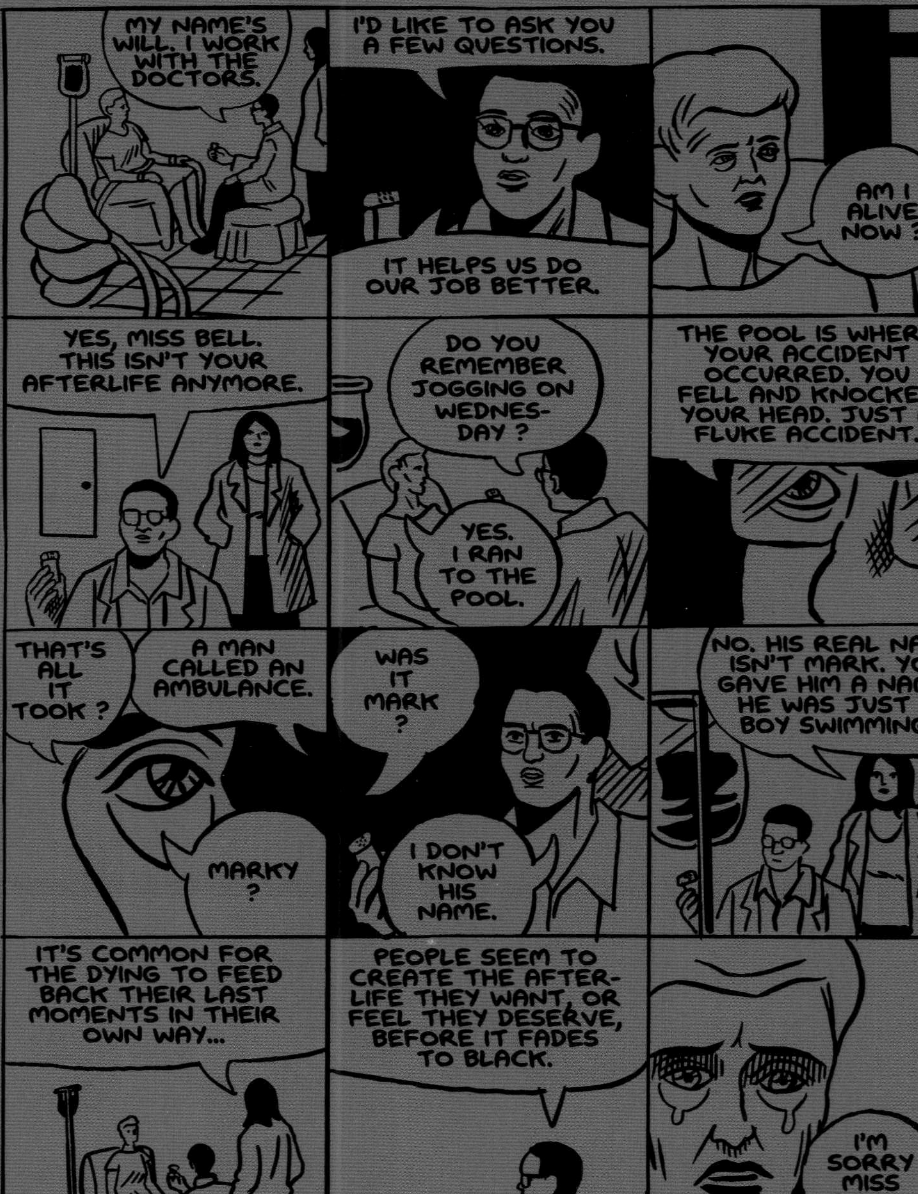
MY NAME'S WILL. I WORK WITH THE DOCTORS.
I'D LIKE TO ASK YOU A FEW QUESTIONS.
IT HELPS US DO OUR JOB BETTER.
AM I ALIVE NOW ?
YES, MISS BELL. THIS ISN'T YOUR AFTERLIFE ANYMORE.
DO YOU REMEMBER JOGGING ON WEDNES-DAY ?
YES. I RAN TO THE POOL.
THE POOL IS WHERE YOUR ACCIDENT OCCURRED. YOU FELL AND KNOCKED YOUR HEAD. JUST A FLUKE ACCIDENT.
THAT'S ALL IT TOOK ?
A MAN CALLED AN AMBULANCE.
MARKY ?
WAS IT MARK ?
I DON'T KNOW HIS NAME.
NO. HIS REAL NAME ISN'T MARK. YOU GAVE HIM A NAME. HE WAS JUST A BOY SWIMMING.
IT'S COMMON FOR THE DYING TO FEED BACK THEIR LAST MOMENTS IN THEIR OWN WAY...
PEOPLE SEEM TO CREATE THE AFTER-LIFE THEY WANT, OR FEEL THEY DESERVE, BEFORE IT FADES TO BLACK.
I'M SORRY MISS BELL...

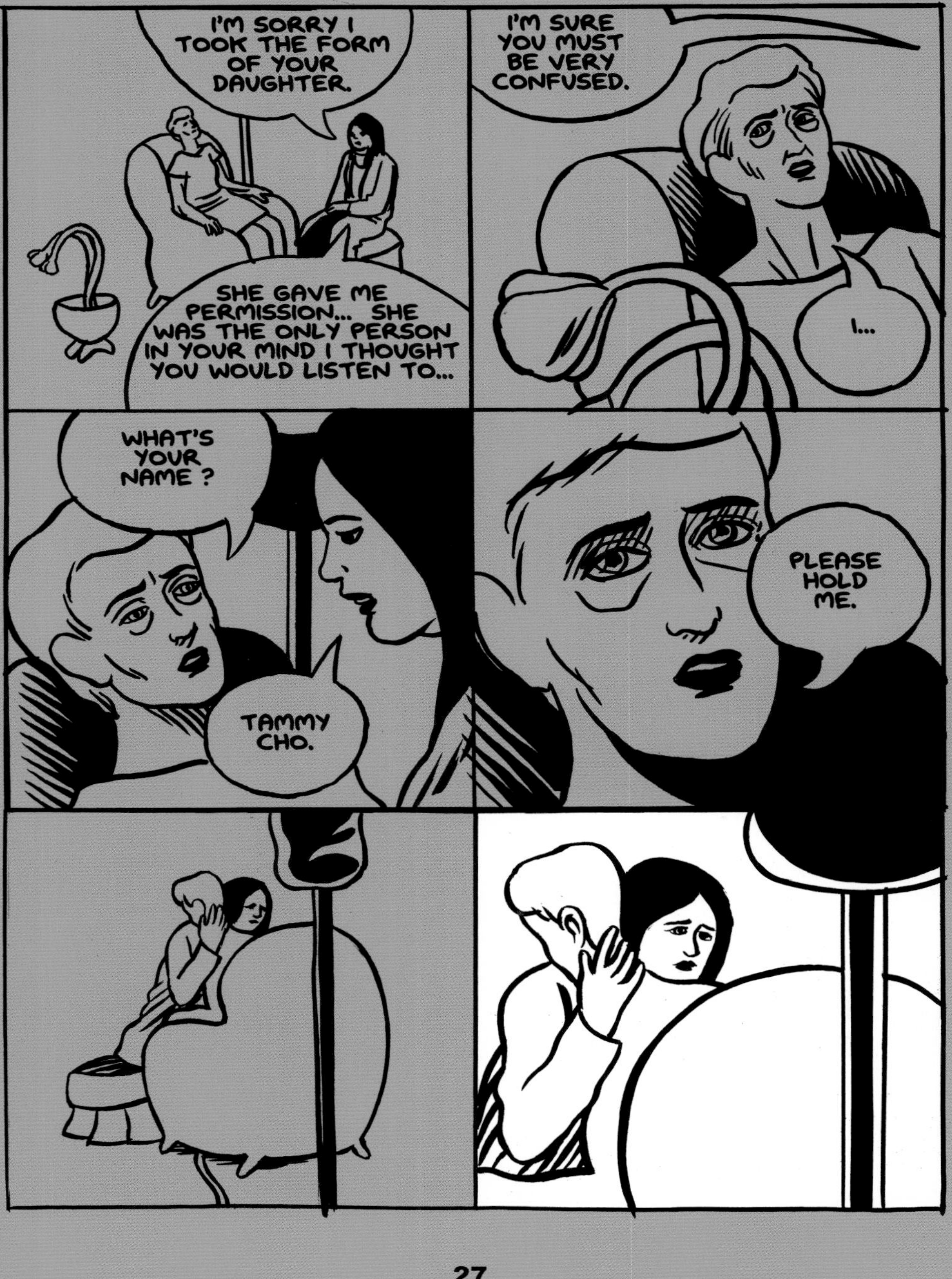
I'M SORRY I TOOK THE FORM OF YOUR DAUGHTER.
SHE GAVE ME PERMISSION... SHE WAS THE ONLY PERSON IN YOUR MIND I THOUGHT YOU WOULD LISTEN TO...
I'M SURE YOU MUST BE VERY CONFUSED.
I...
WHAT'S YOUR NAME ?
TAMMY CHO.
PLEASE HOLD ME.

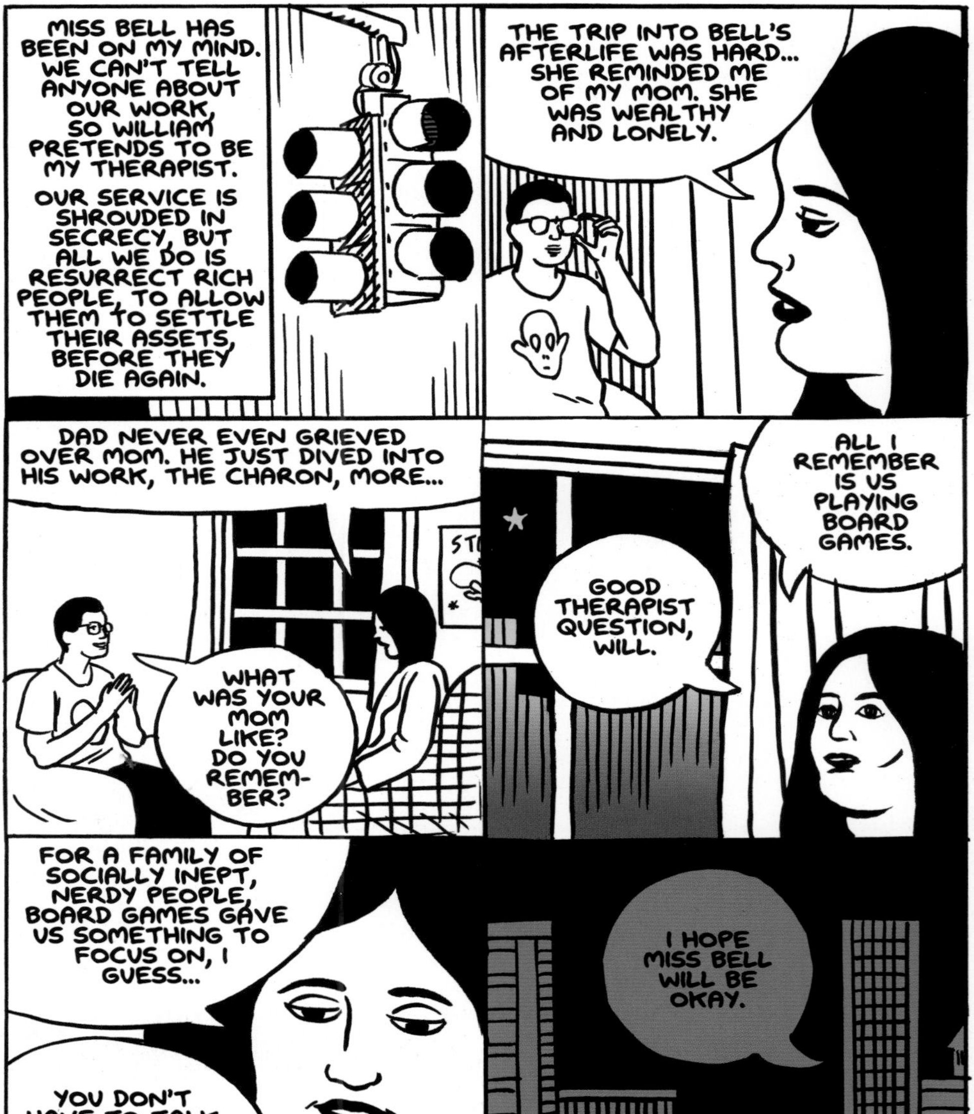
MISS BELL HAS BEEN ON MY MIND. WE CAN'T TELL ANYONE ABOUT OUR WORK, SO WILLIAM PRETENDS TO BE MY THERAPIST.
OUR SERVICE IS SHROUDED IN SECRECY, BUT ALL WE DO IS RESURRECT RICH PEOPLE, TO ALLOW THEM TO SETTLE THEIR ASSETS, BEFORE THEY DIE AGAIN.
THE TRIP INTO BELL'S AFTERLIFE WAS HARD... SHE REMINDED ME OF MY MOM. SHE WAS WEALTHY AND LONELY.
DAD NEVER EVEN GRIEVED OVER MOM. HE JUST DIVED INTO HIS WORK, THE CHARON, MORE...
WHAT WAS YOUR MOM LIKE? DO YOU REMEMBER?
GOOD THERAPIST QUESTION, WILL.
ALL I REMEMBER IS US PLAYING BOARD GAMES.
FOR A FAMILY OF SOCIALLY INEPT, NERDY PEOPLE, BOARD GAMES GAVE US SOMETHING TO FOCUS ON, I GUESS...
YOU DON'T HAVE TO TALK ABOUT HOW YOU FEEL ABOUT EACH OTHER.
I HOPE MISS BELL WILL BE OKAY.

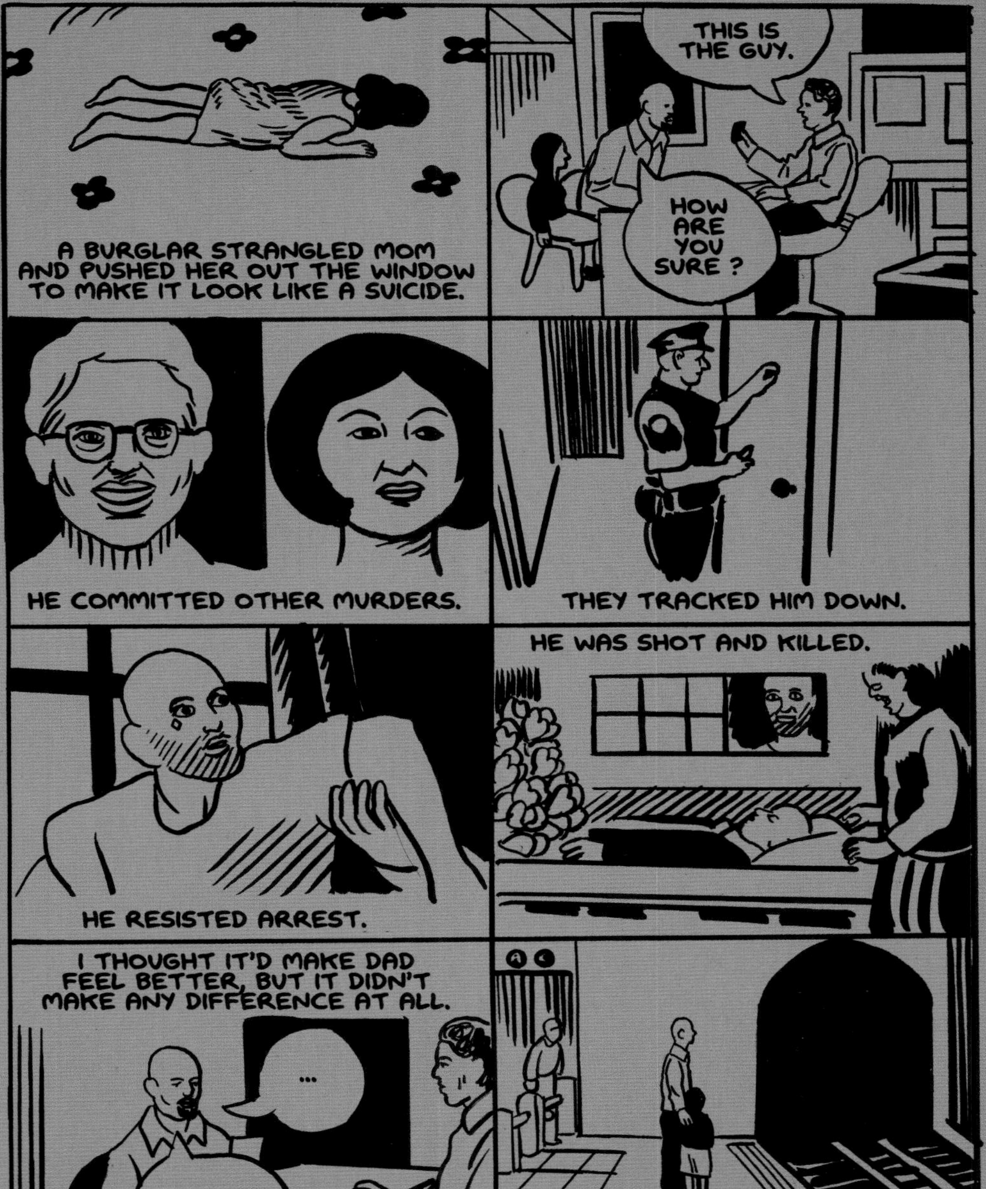
A BURGLAR STRANGLED MOM AND PUSHED HER OUT THE WINDOW TO MAKE IT LOOK LIKE A SUICIDE.
THIS IS THE GUY.
HOW ARE YOU SURE ?
HE COMMITTED OTHER MURDERS.
THEY TRACKED HIM DOWN.
HE RESISTED ARREST.
HE WAS SHOT AND KILLED.
I THOUGHT IT'D MAKE DAD FEEL BETTER, BUT IT DIDN'T MAKE ANY DIFFERENCE AT ALL.
...
OKAY.

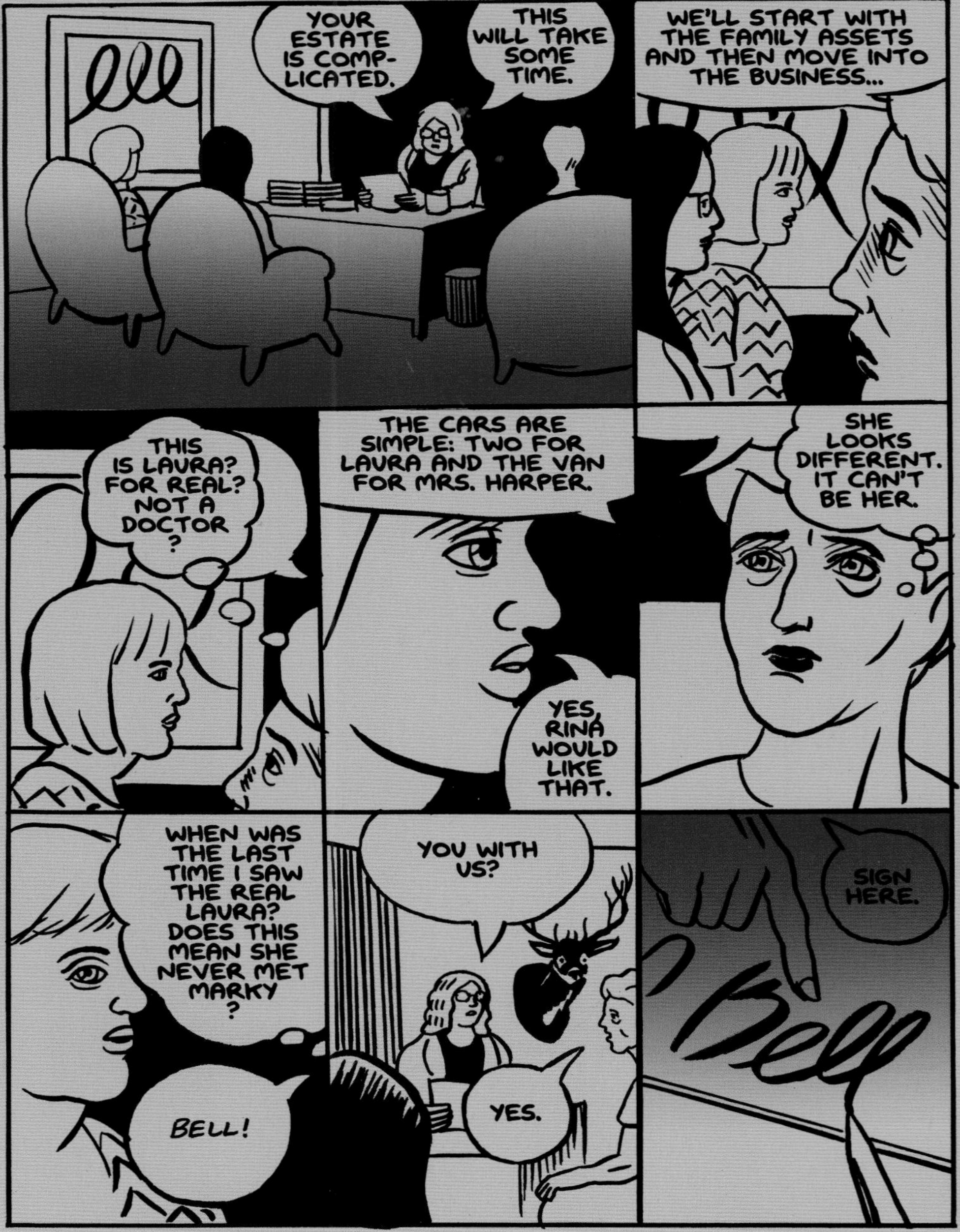
YOUR ESTATE IS COMPLICATED.
THIS WILL TAKE SOME TIME.
WE'LL START WITH THE FAMILY ASSETS AND THEN MOVE INTO THE BUSINESS...
THIS IS LAURA? FOR REAL? NOT A DOCTOR?
THE CARS ARE SIMPLE: TWO FOR LAURA AND THE VAN FOR MRS. HARPER.
YES, RINA WOULD LIKE THAT.
SHE LOOKS DIFFERENT. IT CAN'T BE HER.
WHEN WAS THE LAST TIME I SAW THE REAL LAURA? DOES THIS MEAN SHE NEVER MET MARKY?
BELL!
YOU WITH US?
YES.
SIGN HERE.
Bell

TAMMY HOME FROM WORK

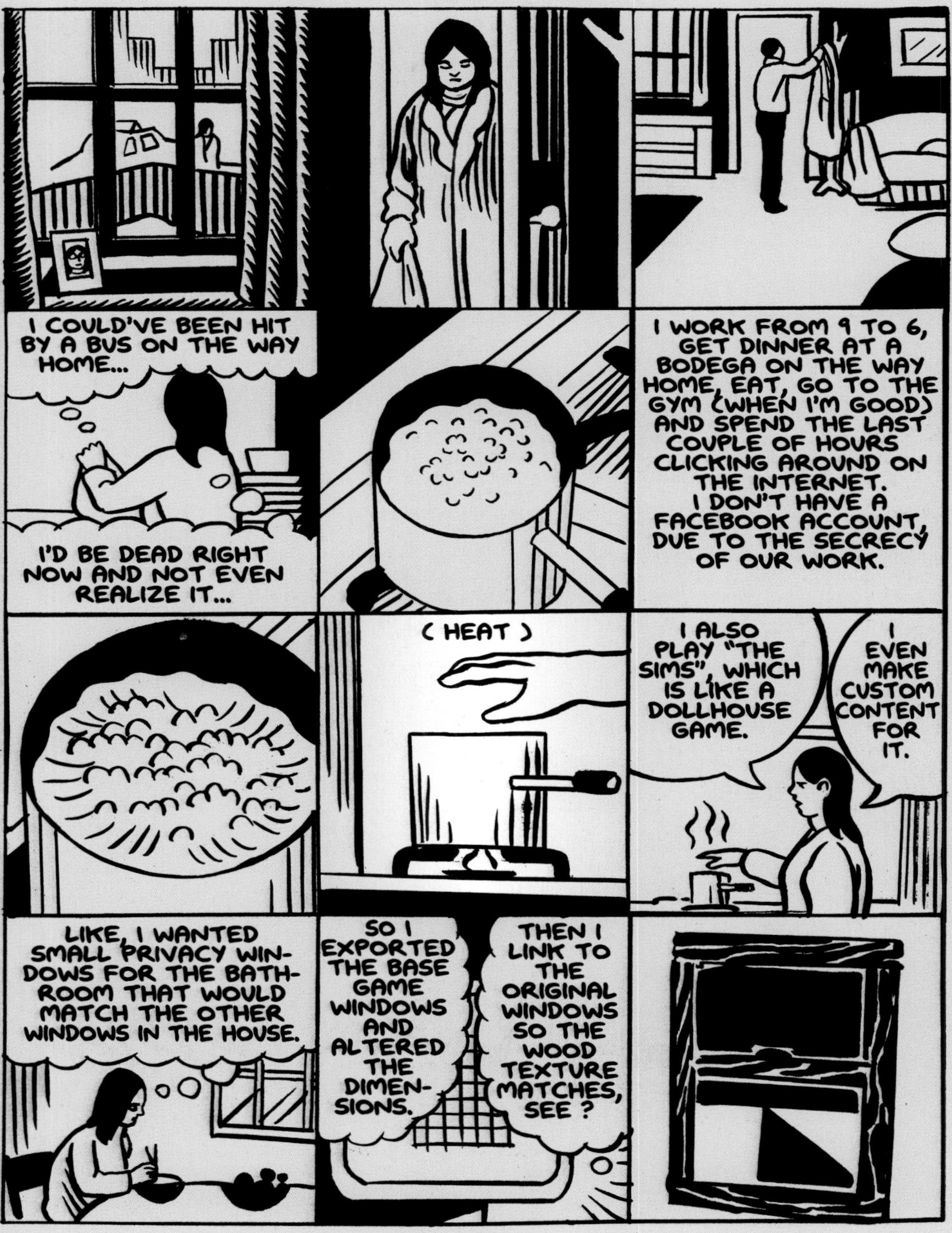
I COULD'VE BEEN HIT BY A BUS ON THE WAY HOME...
I'D BE DEAD RIGHT NOW AND NOT EVEN REALIZE IT...
I WORK FROM 9 TO 6, GET DINNER AT A BODEGA ON THE WAY HOME, EAT, GO TO THE GYM (WHEN I'M GOOD) AND SPEND THE LAST COUPLE OF HOURS CLICKING AROUND ON THE INTERNET. I DON'T HAVE A FACEBOOK ACCOUNT, DUE TO THE SECRECY OF OUR WORK.
(HEAT)
I ALSO PLAY "THE SIMS", WHICH IS LIKE A DOLLHOUSE GAME.
I EVEN MAKE CUSTOM CONTENT FOR IT.
LIKE, I WANTED SMALL PRIVACY WINDOWS FOR THE BATHROOM THAT WOULD MATCH THE OTHER WINDOWS IN THE HOUSE.
SO I EXPORTED THE BASE GAME WINDOWS AND ALTERED THE DIMENSIONS.
THEN I LINK TO THE ORIGINAL WINDOWS SO THE WOOD TEXTURE MATCHES, SEE ?

TAMMY'S FATHER AKA "DR. NO"

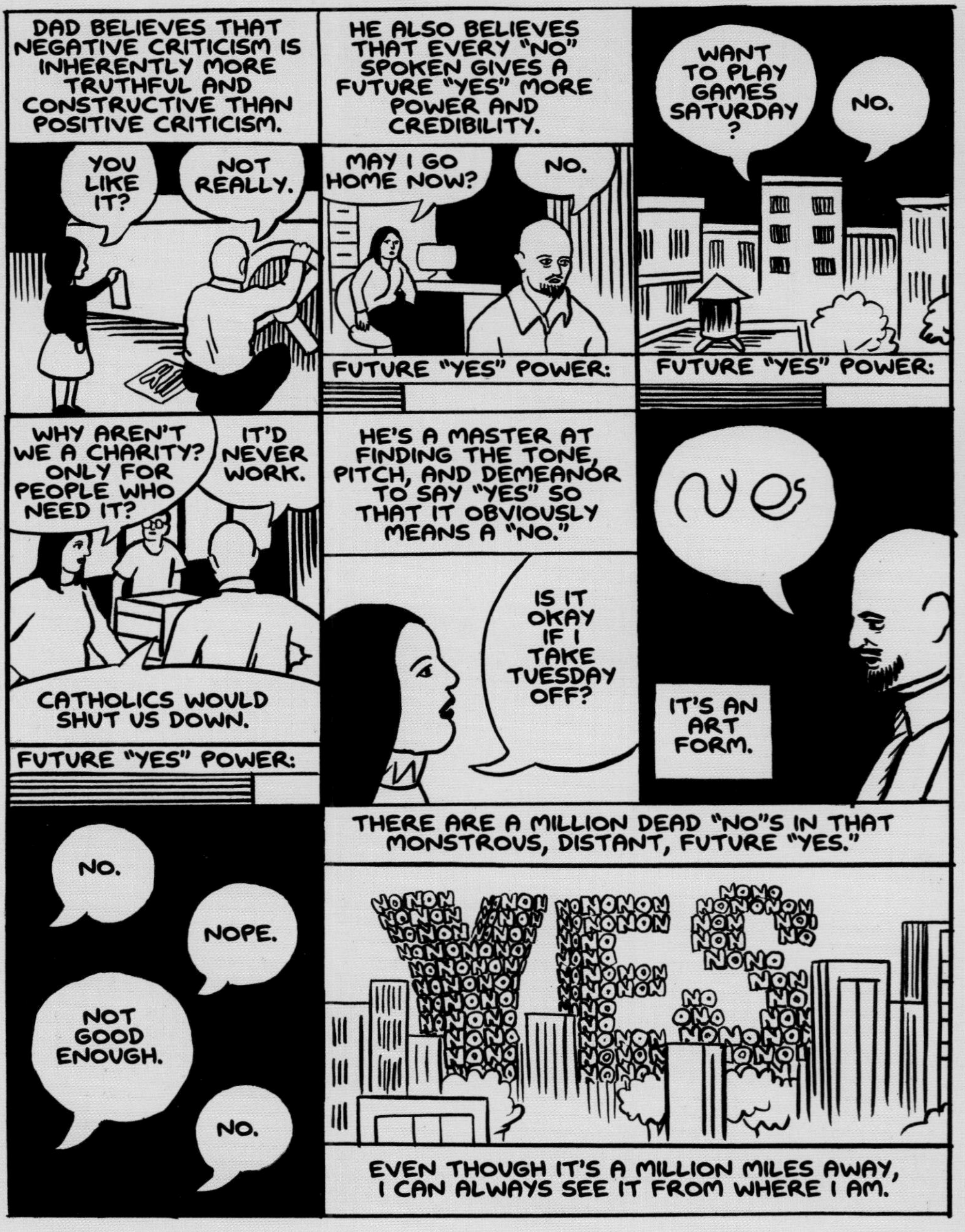

DAD BELIEVES THAT NEGATIVE CRITICISM IS INHERENTLY MORE TRUTHFUL AND CONSTRUCTIVE THAN POSITIVE CRITICISM.
YOU LIKE IT?
NOT REALLY.
HE ALSO BELIEVES THAT EVERY "NO" SPOKEN GIVES A FUTURE "YES" MORE POWER AND CREDIBILITY.
MAY I GO HOME NOW?
NO.
FUTURE "YES" POWER:
WANT TO PLAY GAMES SATURDAY?
NO.
FUTURE "YES" POWER:
WHY AREN'T WE A CHARITY? ONLY FOR PEOPLE WHO NEED IT?
IT'D NEVER WORK.
CATHOLICS WOULD SHUT US DOWN.
FUTURE "YES" POWER:
HE'S A MASTER AT FINDING THE TONE, PITCH, AND DEMEANOR TO SAY "YES" SO THAT IT OBVIOUSLY MEANS A "NO."
IS IT OKAY IF I TAKE TUESDAY OFF?
Yes
IT'S AN ART FORM.
NO.
NOPE.
NOT GOOD ENOUGH.
NO.
THERE ARE A MILLION DEAD "NO"S IN THAT MONSTROUS, DISTANT, FUTURE "YES."
YES
EVEN THOUGH IT'S A MILLION MILES AWAY, I CAN ALWAYS SEE IT FROM WHERE I AM.

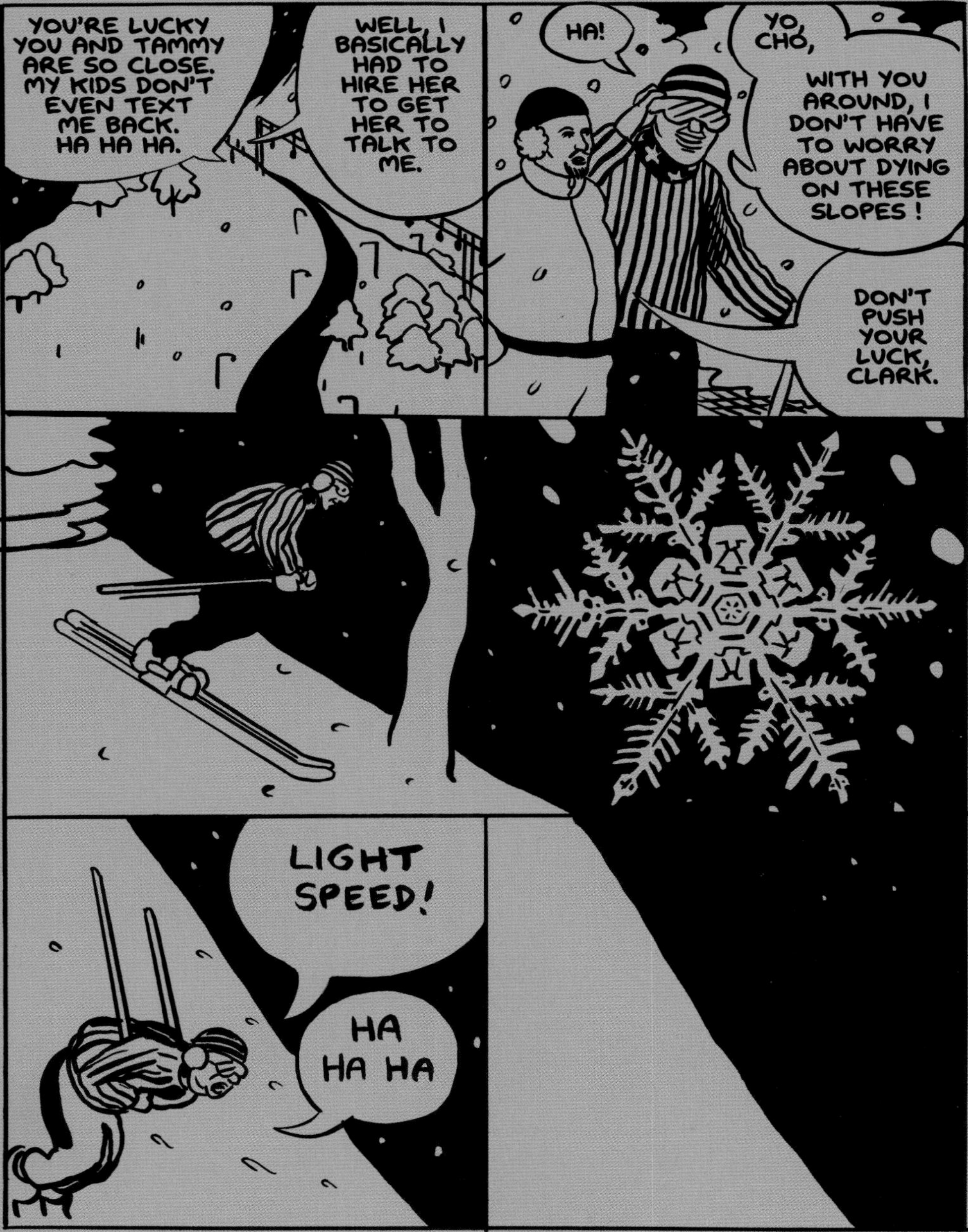
YOU'RE LUCKY YOU AND TAMMY ARE SO CLOSE. MY KIDS DON'T EVEN TEXT ME BACK. HA HA HA.
WELL, I BASICALLY HAD TO HIRE HER TO GET HER TO TALK TO ME.
HA!
YO, CHO,
WITH YOU AROUND, I DON'T HAVE TO WORRY ABOUT DYING ON THESE SLOPES !
DON'T PUSH YOUR LUCK, CLARK.
LIGHT SPEED!
HA HA HA

35

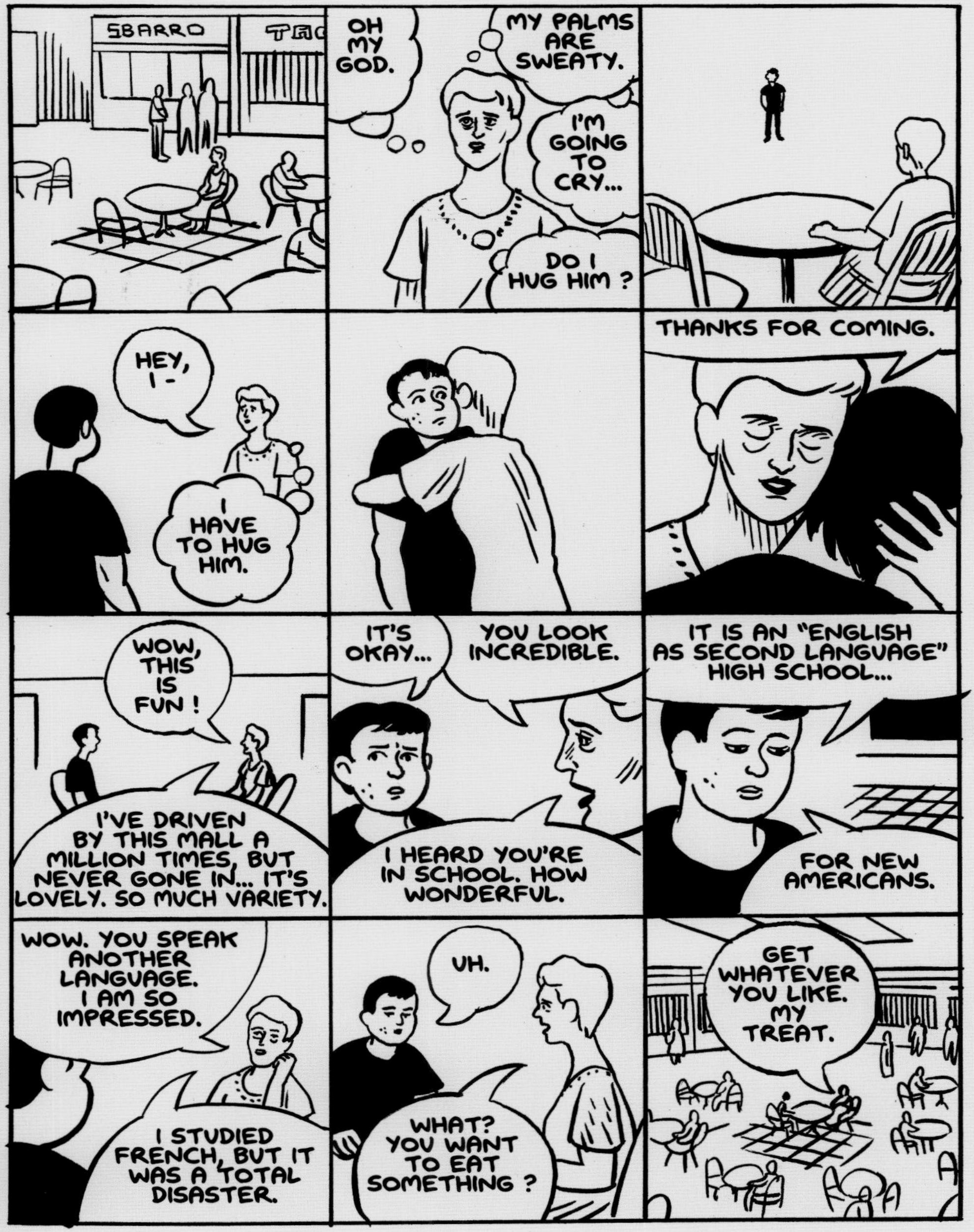
SBARRO
OH MY GOD.
MY PALMS ARE SWEATY.
I'M GOING TO CRY...
DO I HUG HIM ?
HEY, I -
I HAVE TO HUG HIM.
THANKS FOR COMING.
WOW, THIS IS FUN !
I'VE DRIVEN BY THIS MALL A MILLION TIMES, BUT NEVER GONE IN... IT'S LOVELY. SO MUCH VARIETY.
IT'S OKAY...
YOU LOOK INCREDIBLE.
I HEARD YOU'RE IN SCHOOL. HOW WONDERFUL.
IT IS AN "ENGLISH AS SECOND LANGUAGE" HIGH SCHOOL...
FOR NEW AMERICANS.
WOW. YOU SPEAK ANOTHER LANGUAGE. I AM SO IMPRESSED.
I STUDIED FRENCH, BUT IT WAS A TOTAL DISASTER.
UH.
WHAT? YOU WANT TO EAT SOMETHING ?
GET WHATEVER YOU LIKE. MY TREAT.

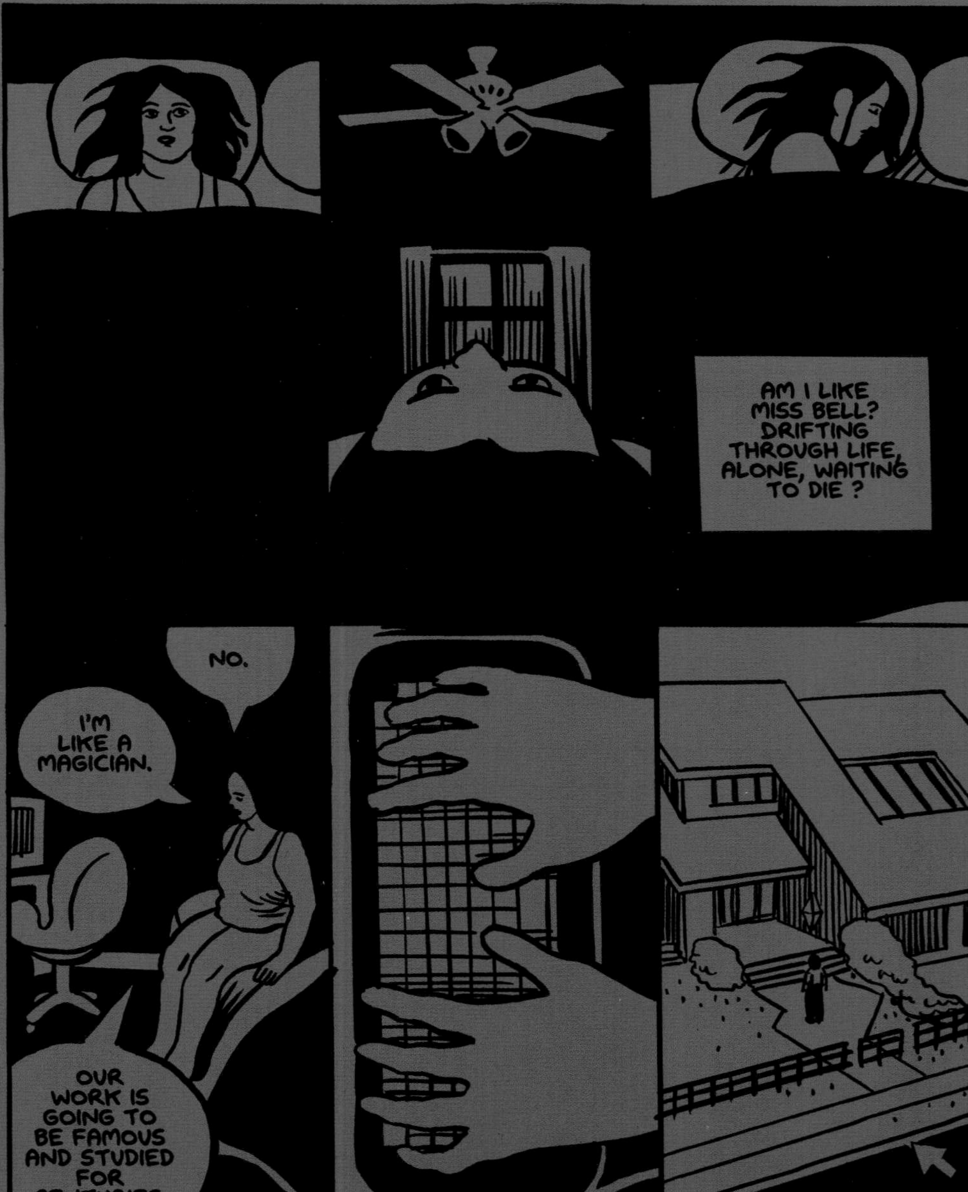
AM I LIKE MISS BELL? DRIFTING THROUGH LIFE, ALONE, WAITING TO DIE ?
NO.
I'M LIKE A MAGICIAN.
OUR WORK IS GOING TO BE FAMOUS AND STUDIED FOR CENTURIES.

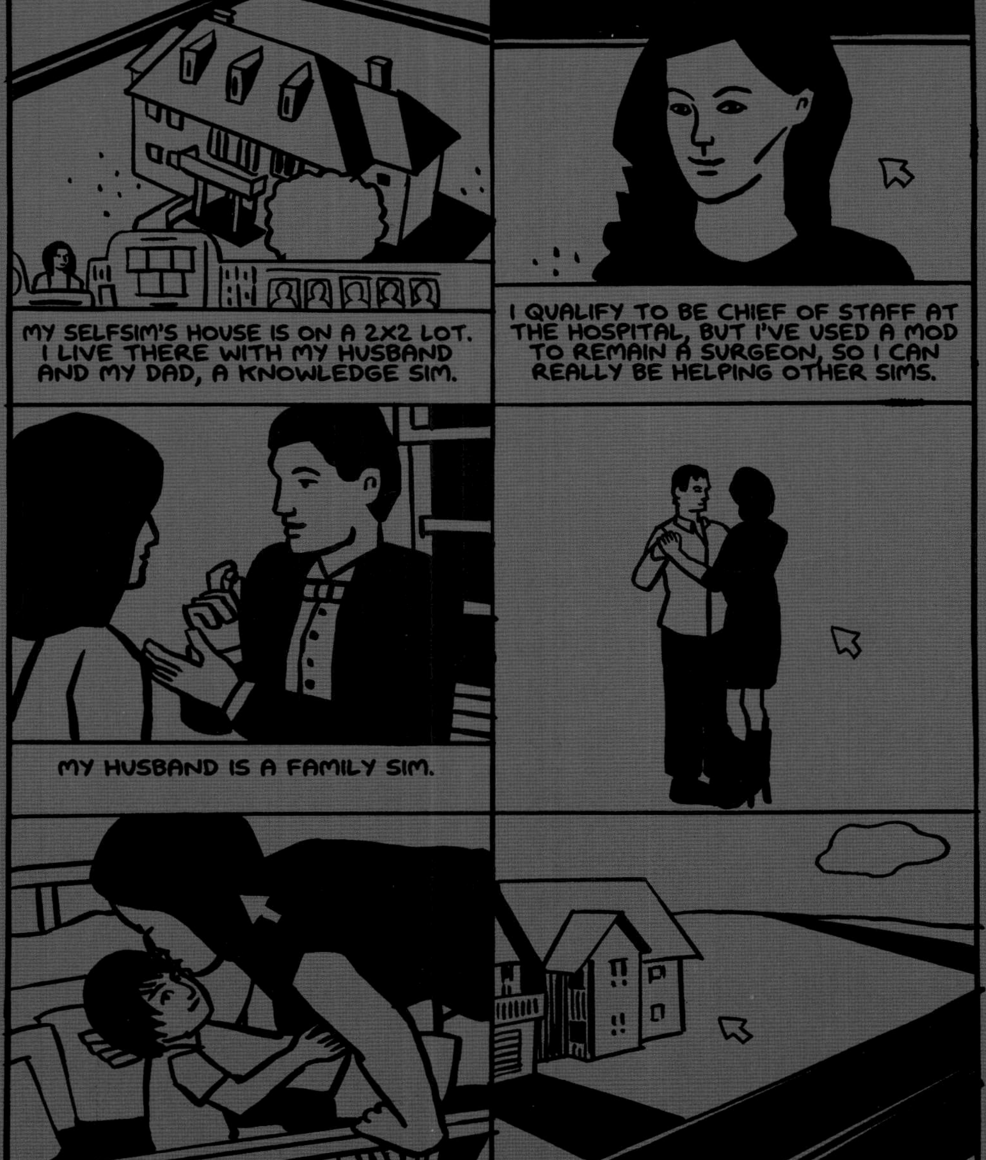
MY SELFSIM'S HOUSE IS ON A 2X2 LOT. I LIVE THERE WITH MY HUSBAND AND MY DAD, A KNOWLEDGE SIM.
I QUALIFY TO BE CHIEF OF STAFF AT THE HOSPITAL, BUT I'VE USED A MOD TO REMAIN A SURGEON, SO I CAN REALLY BE HELPING OTHER SIMS.
MY HUSBAND IS A FAMILY SIM.

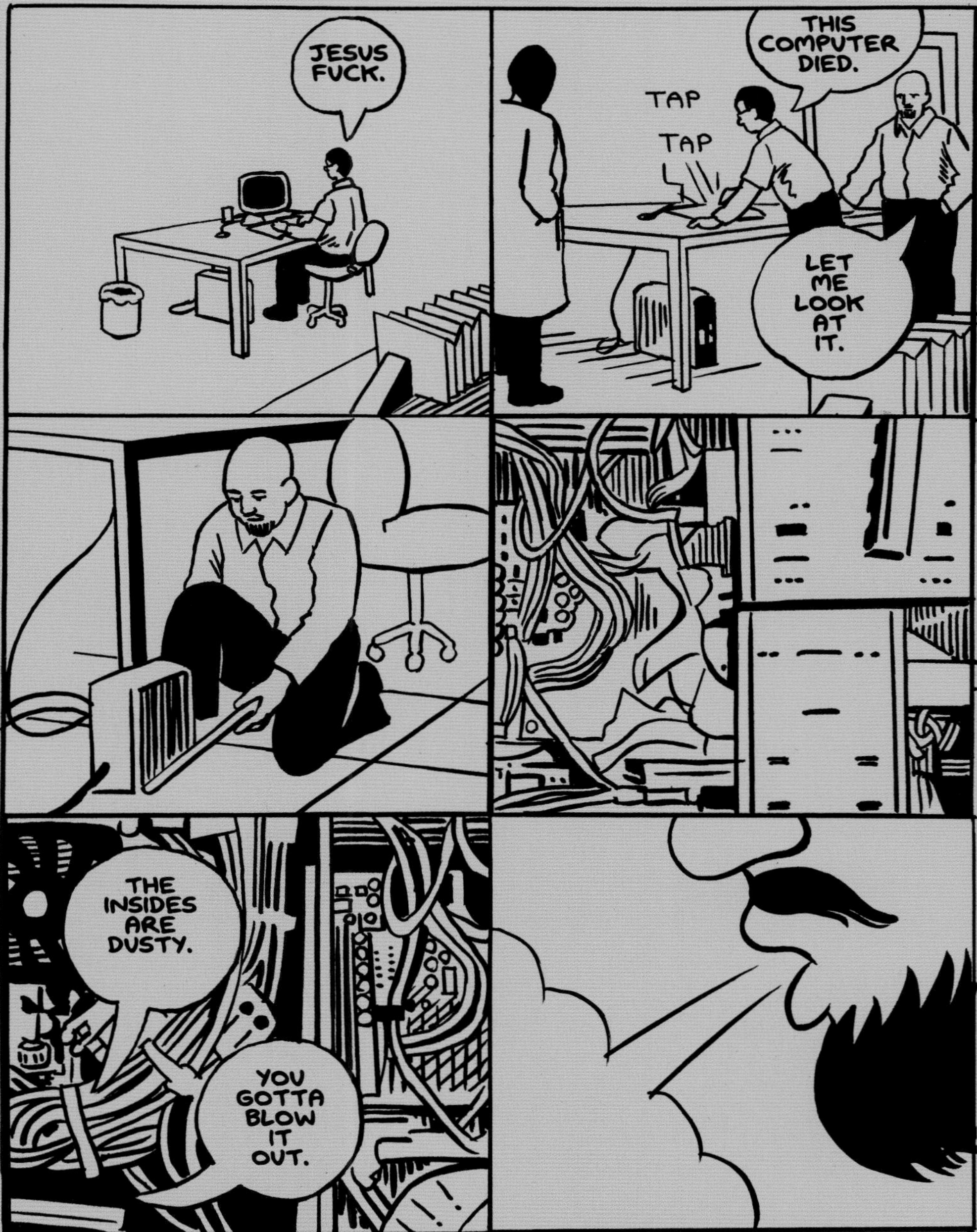
JESUS FUCK.
TAP
TAP
THIS COMPUTER DIED.
LET ME LOOK AT IT.
THE INSIDES ARE DUSTY.
YOU GOTTA BLOW IT OUT.

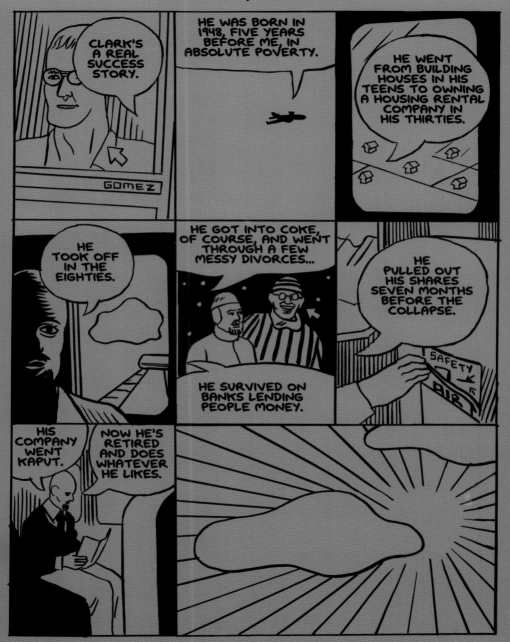

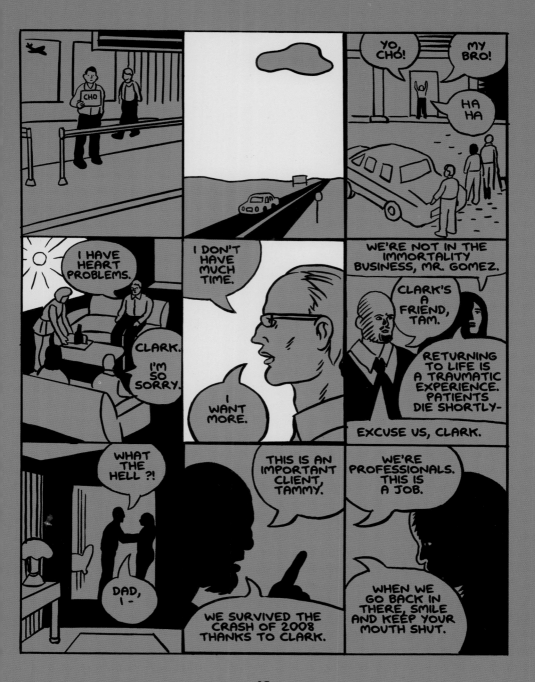

46

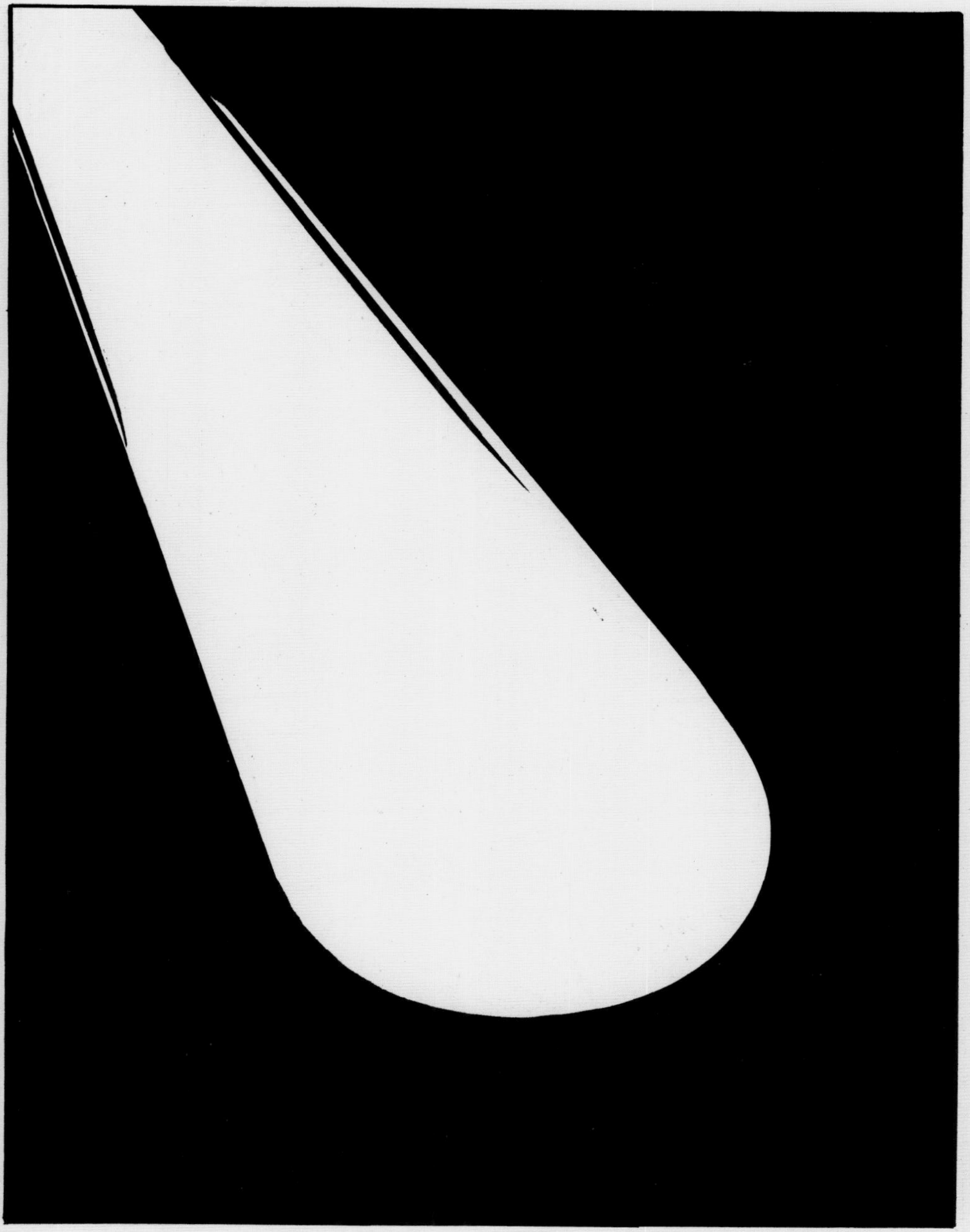

ON THE WAY TO WORK

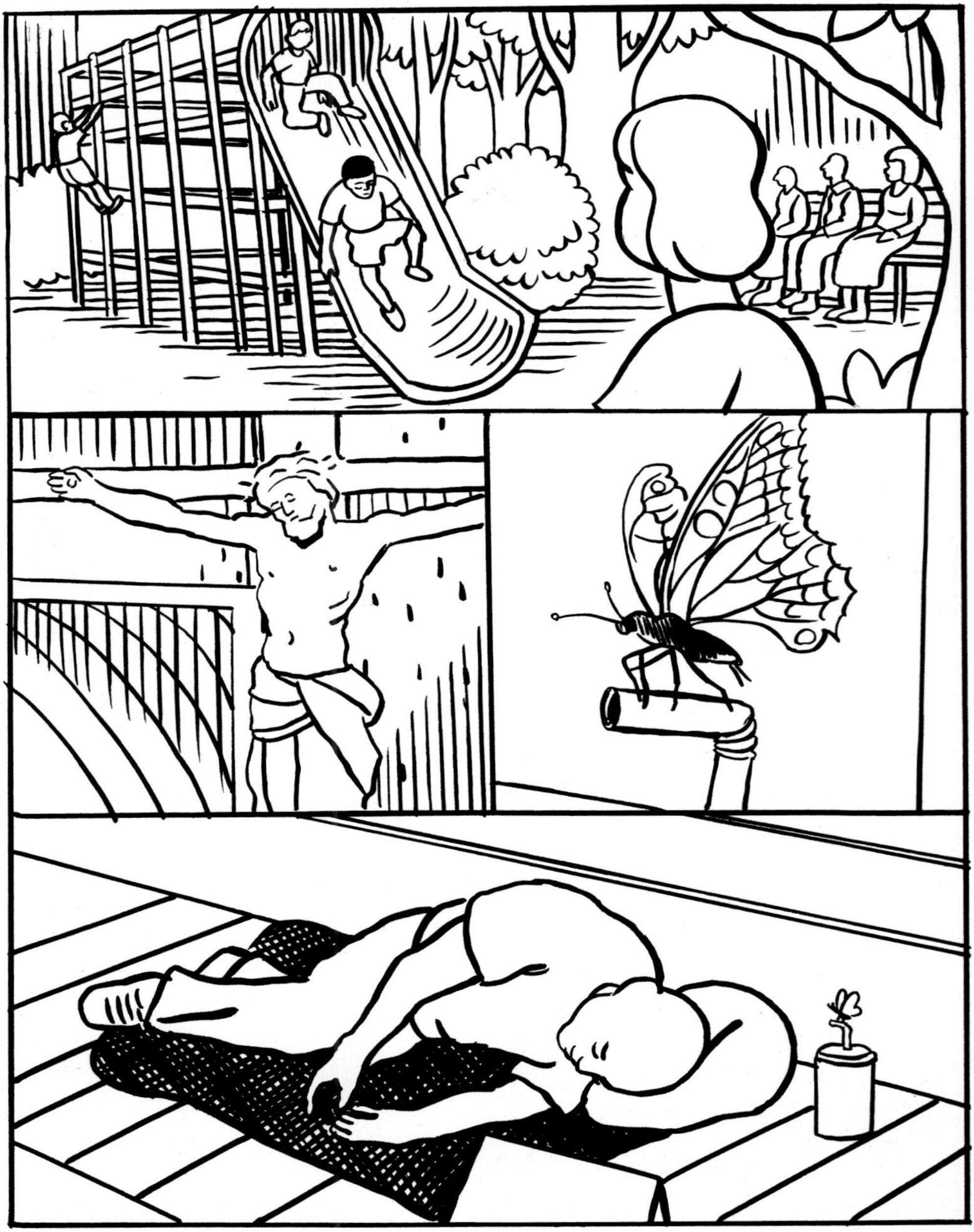

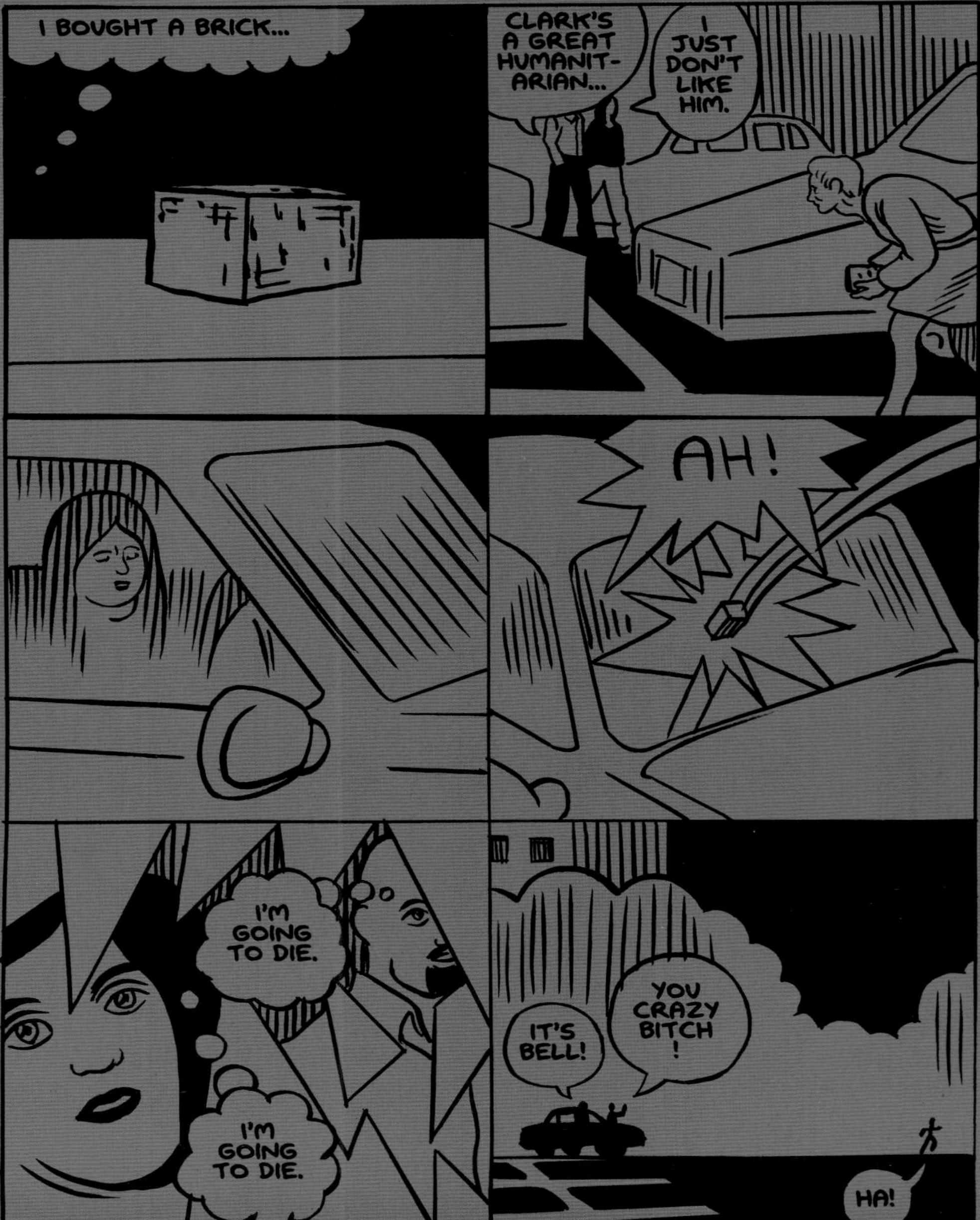
I BOUGHT A BRICK...
CLARK'S A GREAT HUMANITARIAN...
I JUST DON'T LIKE HIM.
AH!
I'M GOING TO DIE.
I'M GOING TO DIE.
IT'S BELL!
YOU CRAZY BITCH!
HA!

53

54

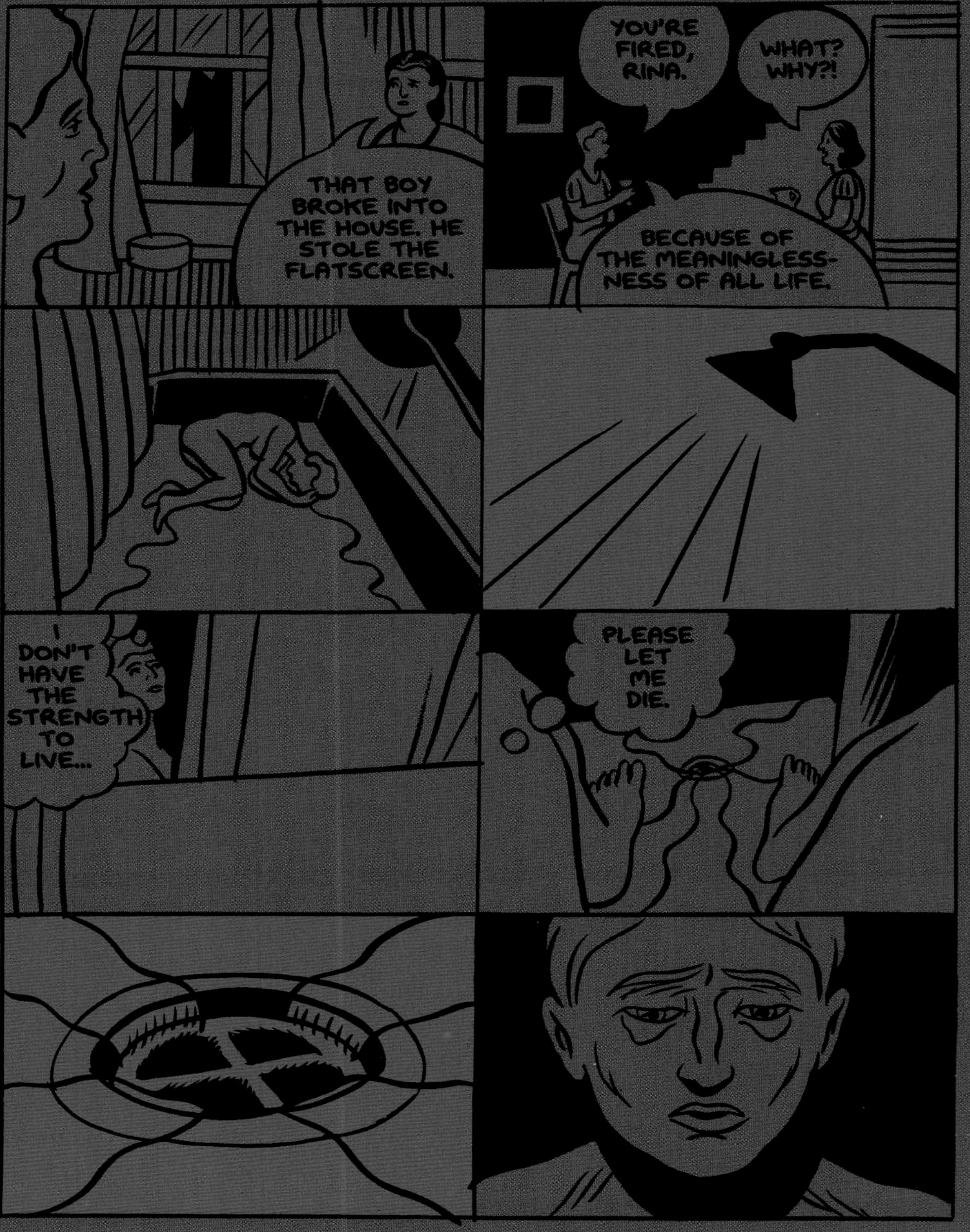
THAT BOY BROKE INTO THE HOUSE. HE STOLE THE FLATSCREEN.
YOU'RE FIRED, RINA.
WHAT? WHY?!
BECAUSE OF THE MEANINGLESS-NESS OF ALL LIFE.
I DON'T HAVE THE STRENGTH TO LIVE...
PLEASE LET ME DIE.

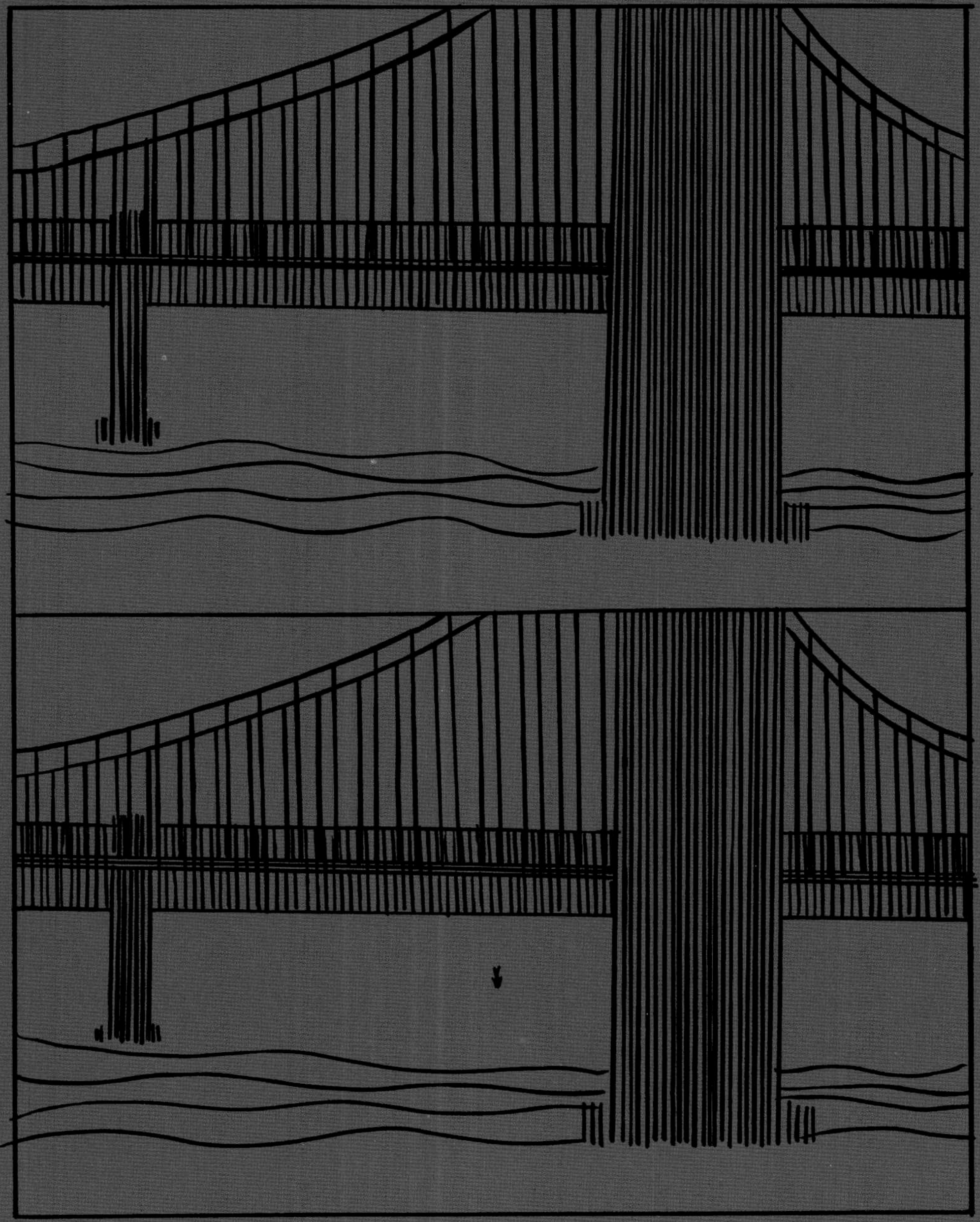

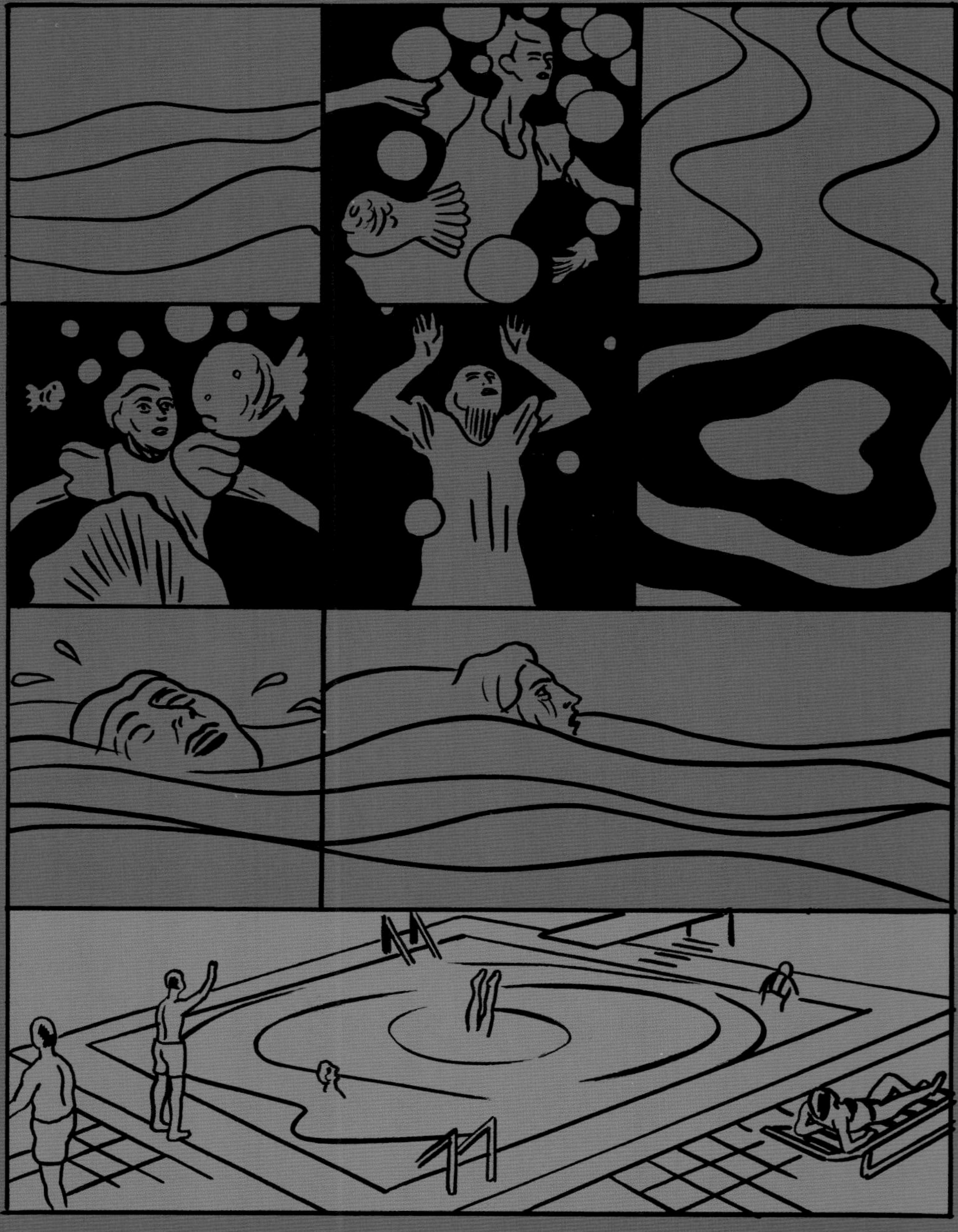

61

62

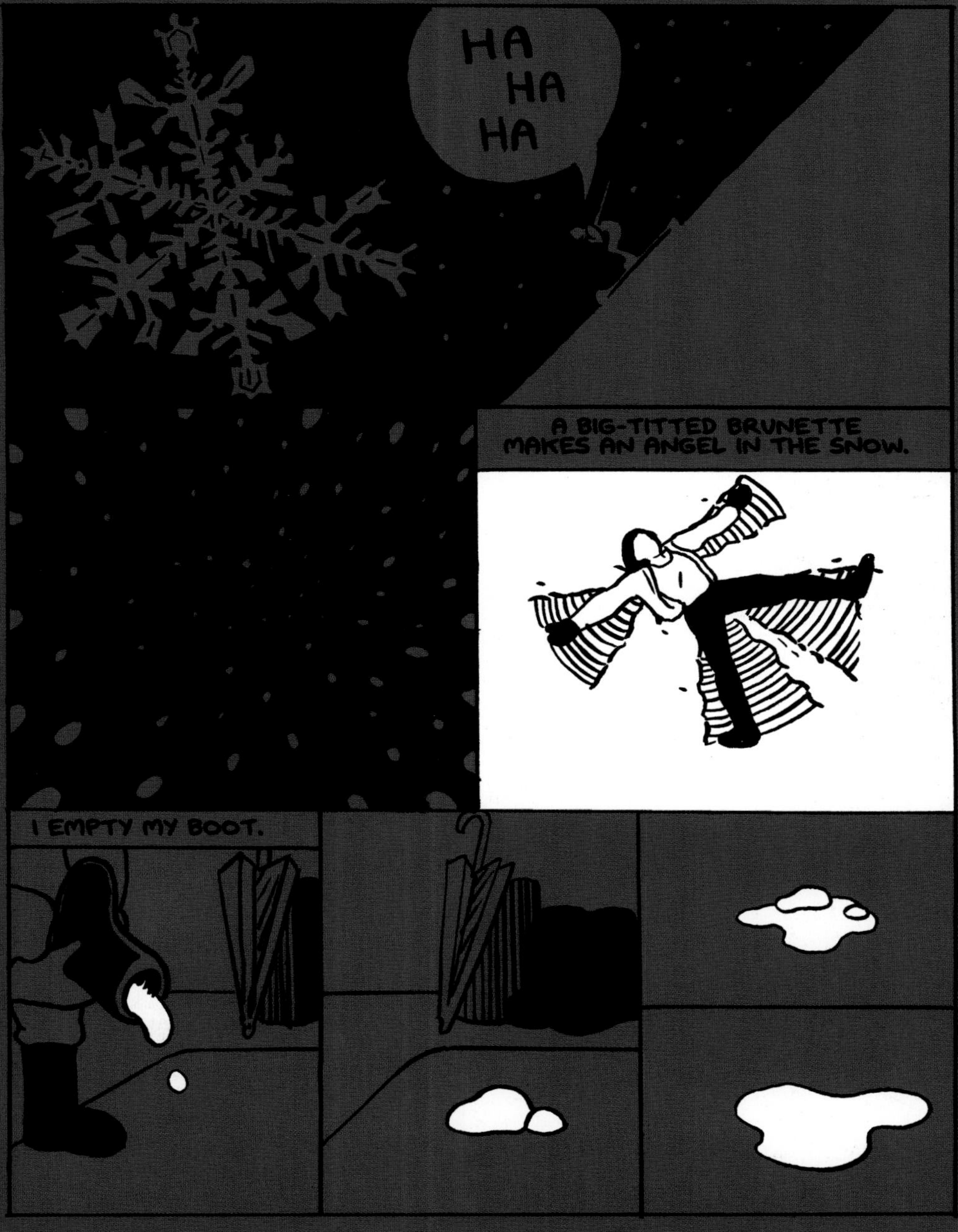
HA
HA
HA
A BIG-TITTED BRUNETTE MAKES AN ANGEL IN THE SNOW.
I EMPTY MY BOOT.

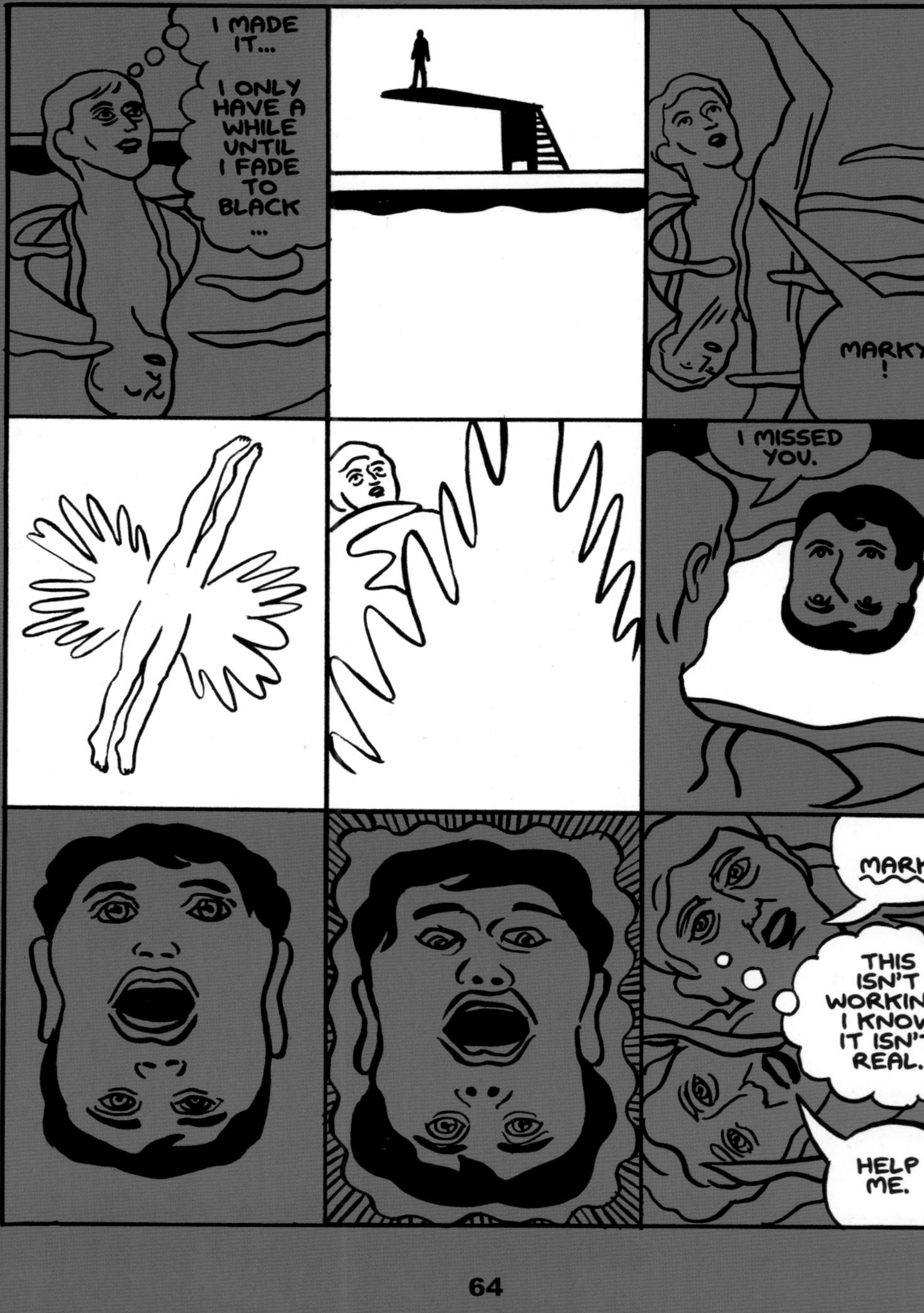
I MADE IT...
I ONLY HAVE A WHILE UNTIL I FADE TO BLACK ...
MARKY!
I MISSED YOU.
MARK?
THIS ISN'T WORKING. I KNOW IT ISN'T REAL.
HELP ME.

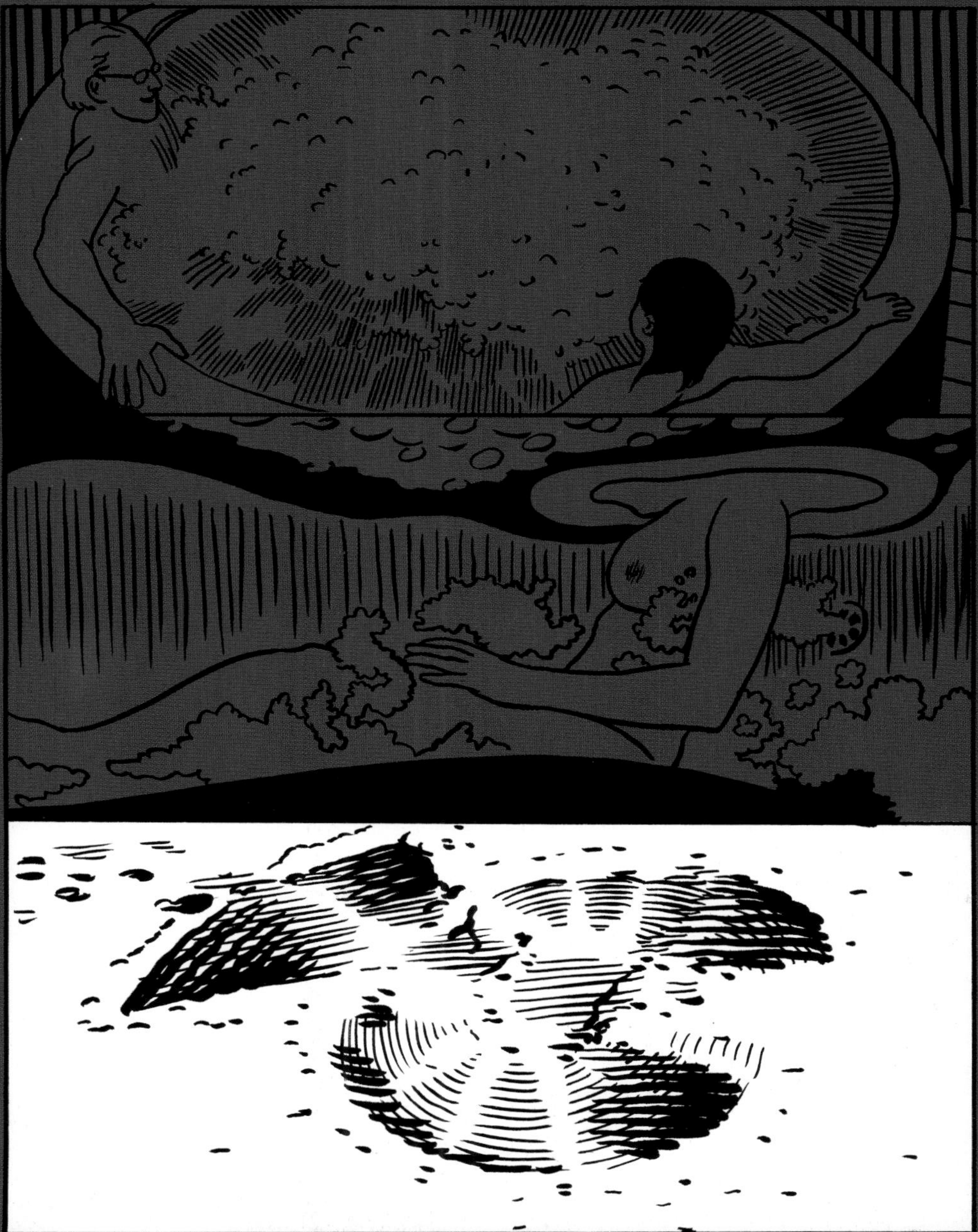

67

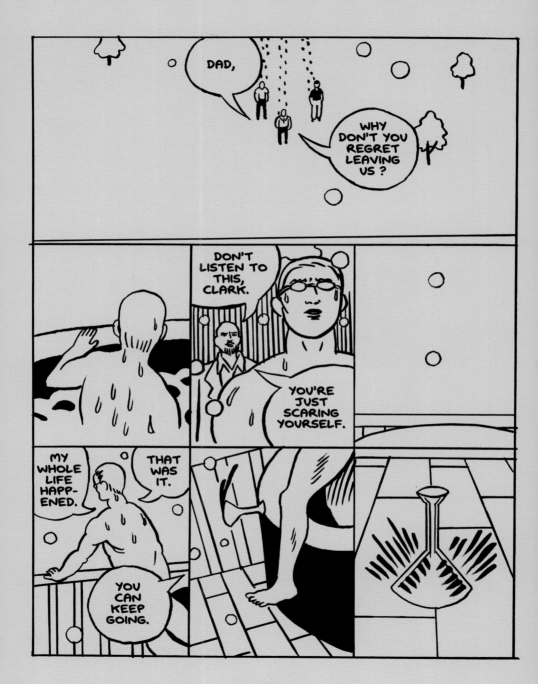

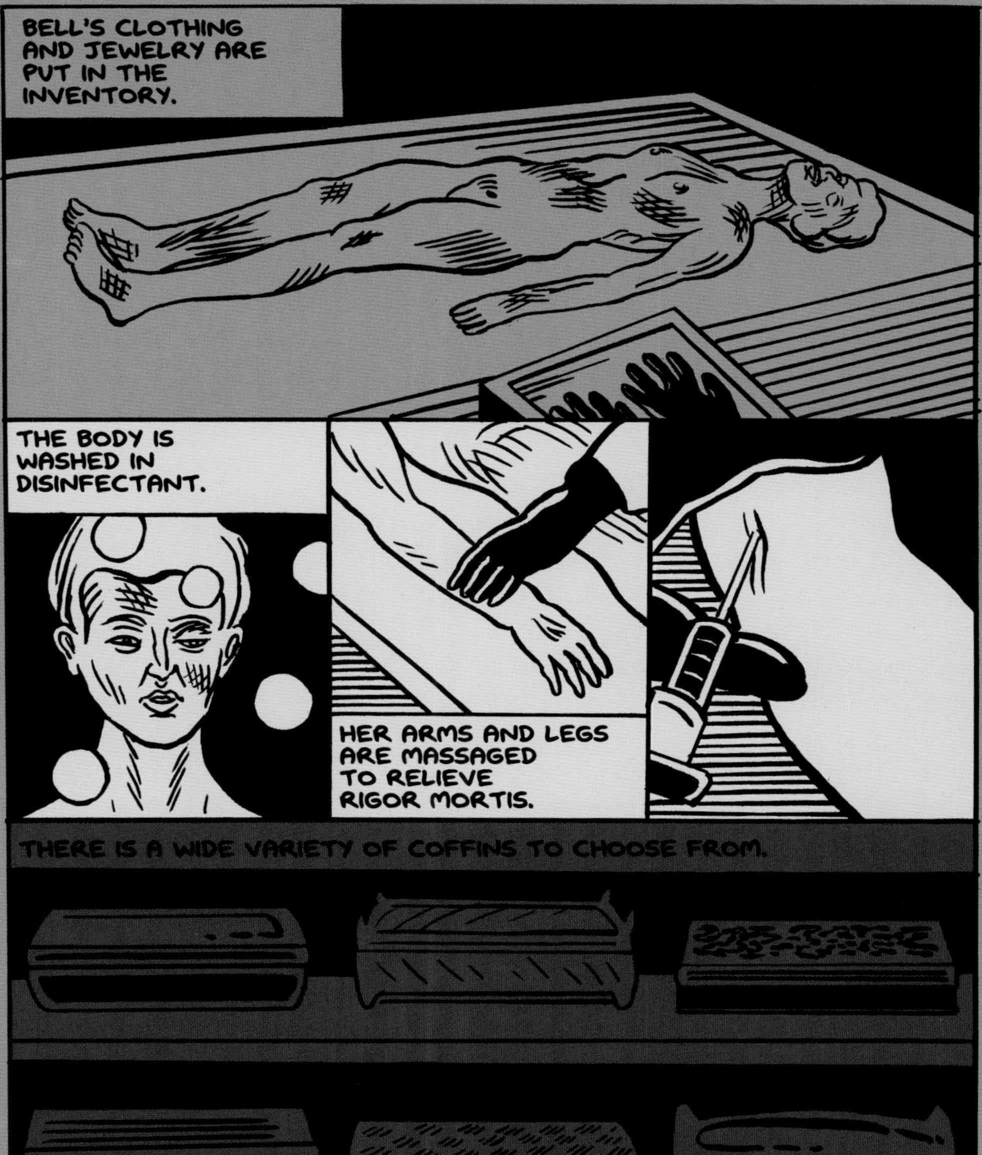
BELL'S CLOTHING AND JEWELRY ARE PUT IN THE INVENTORY.
THE BODY IS WASHED IN DISINFECTANT.
HER ARMS AND LEGS ARE MASSAGED TO RELIEVE RIGOR MORTIS.
THERE IS A WIDE VARIETY OF COFFINS TO CHOOSE FROM.

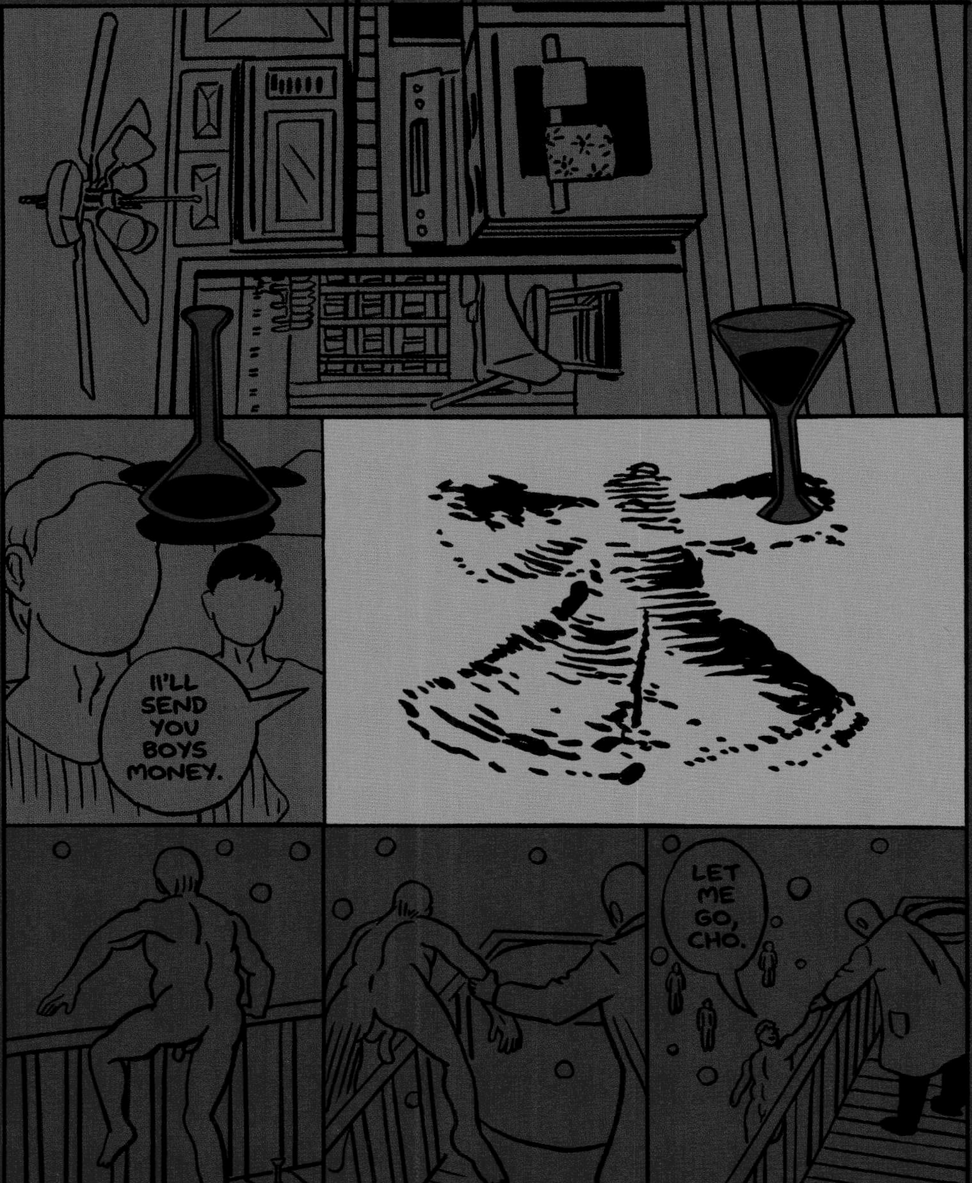
I'LL SEND YOU BOYS MONEY.
LET ME GO, CHO.

74

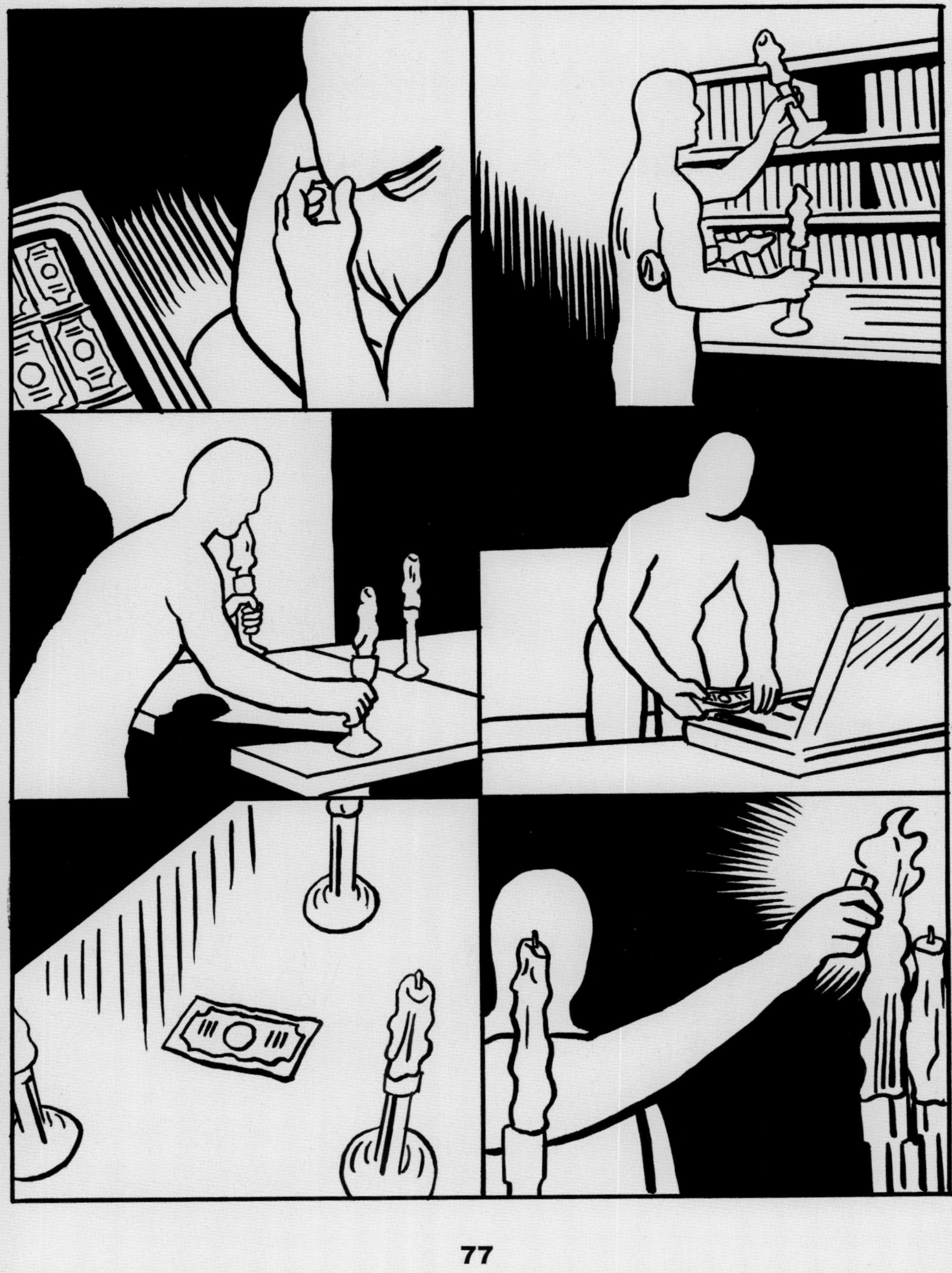

78

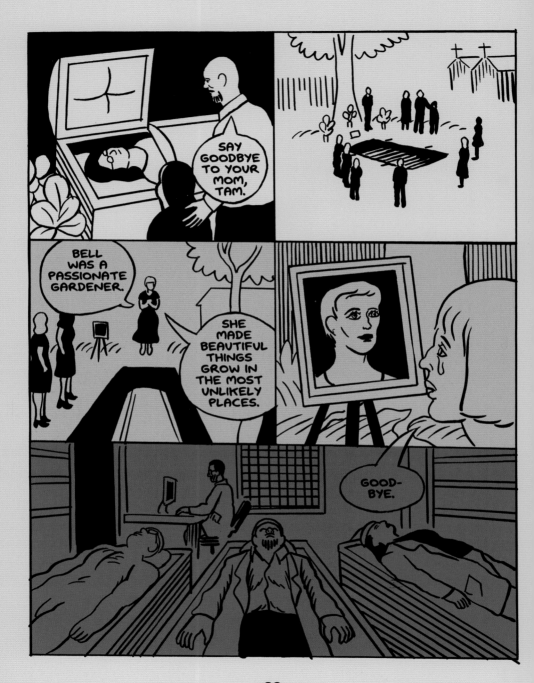

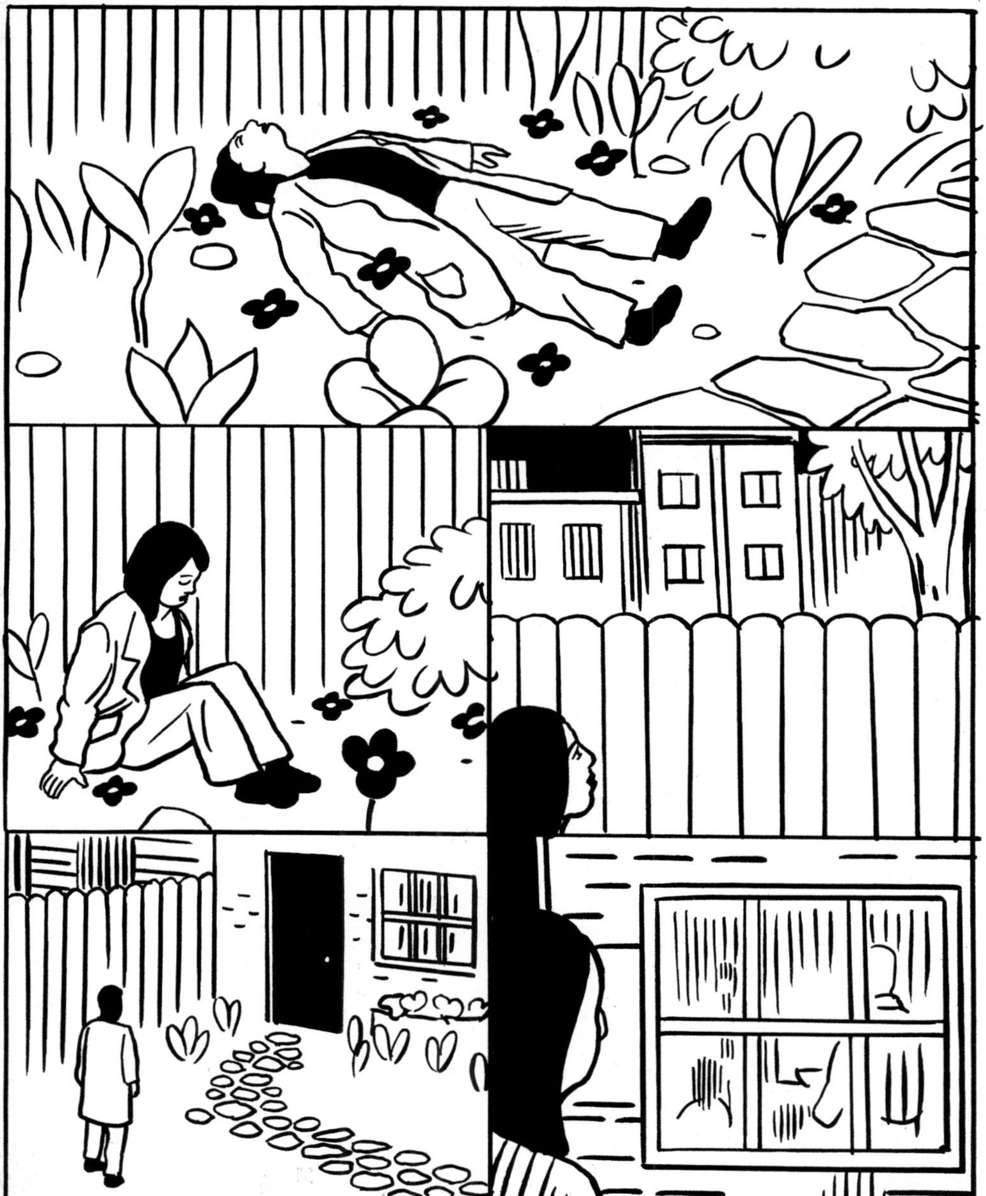

84

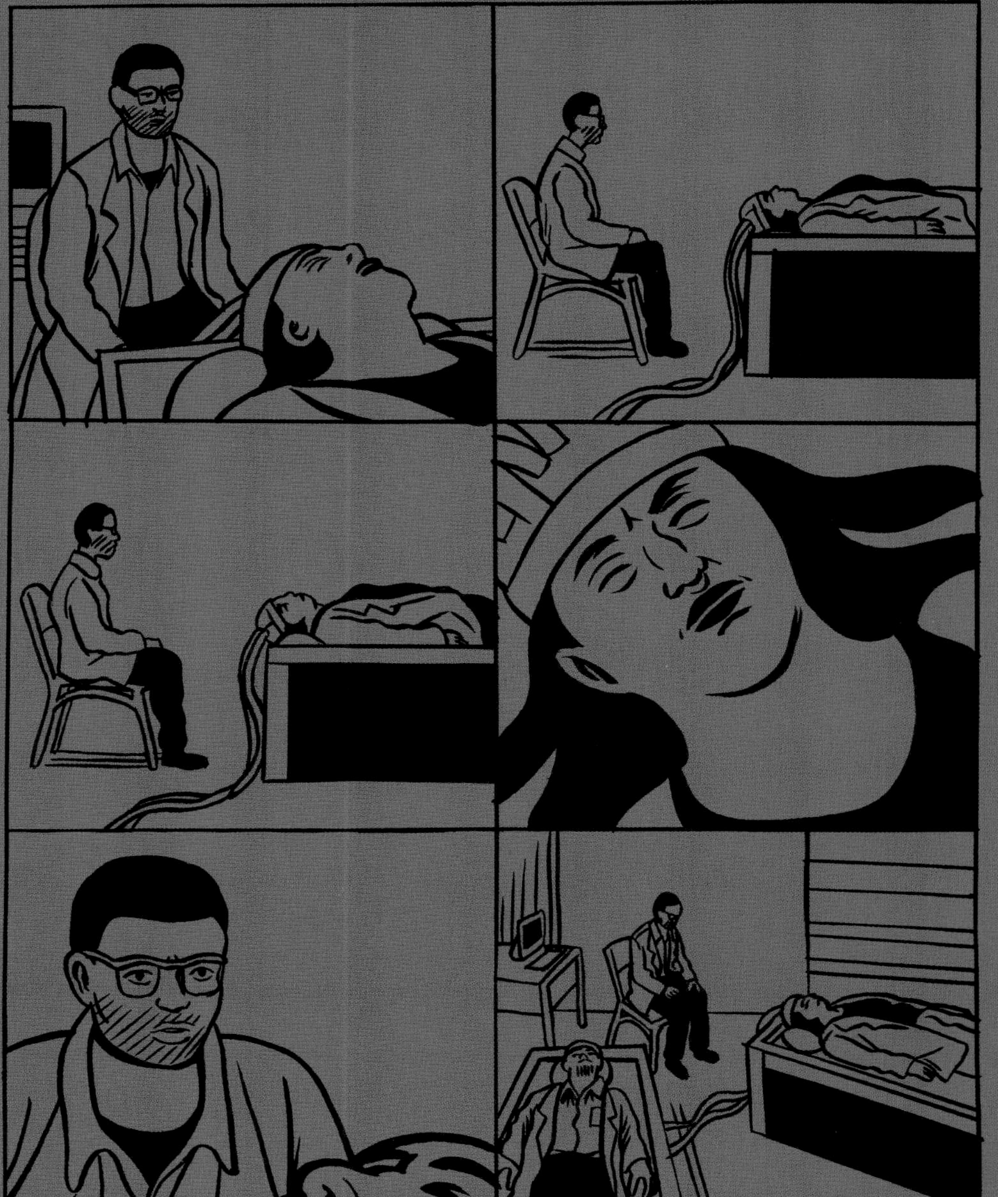

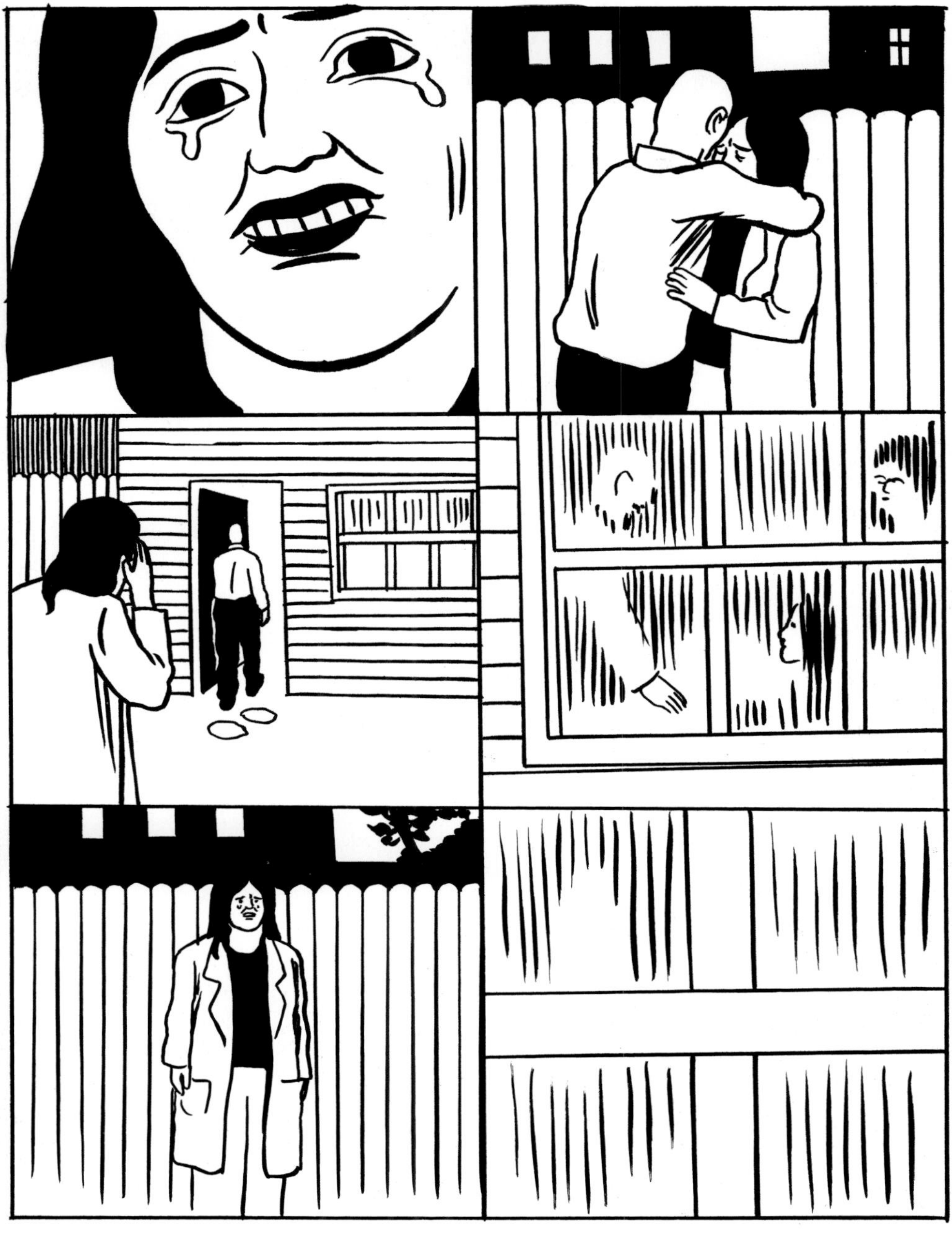

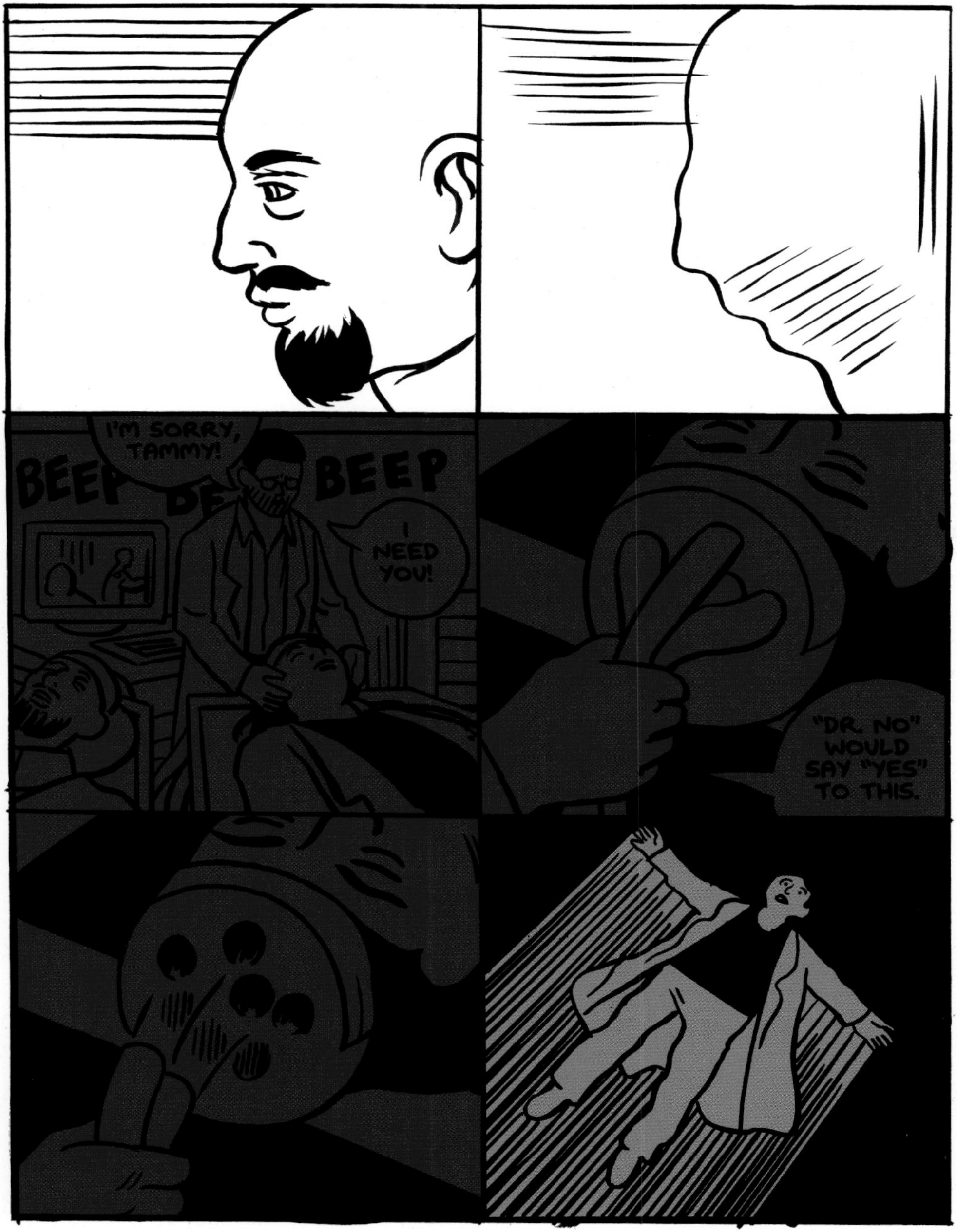
I'M SORRY, TAMMY!
BEEP
BEEP
I NEED YOU!
"DR. NO" WOULD SAY "YES" TO THIS.

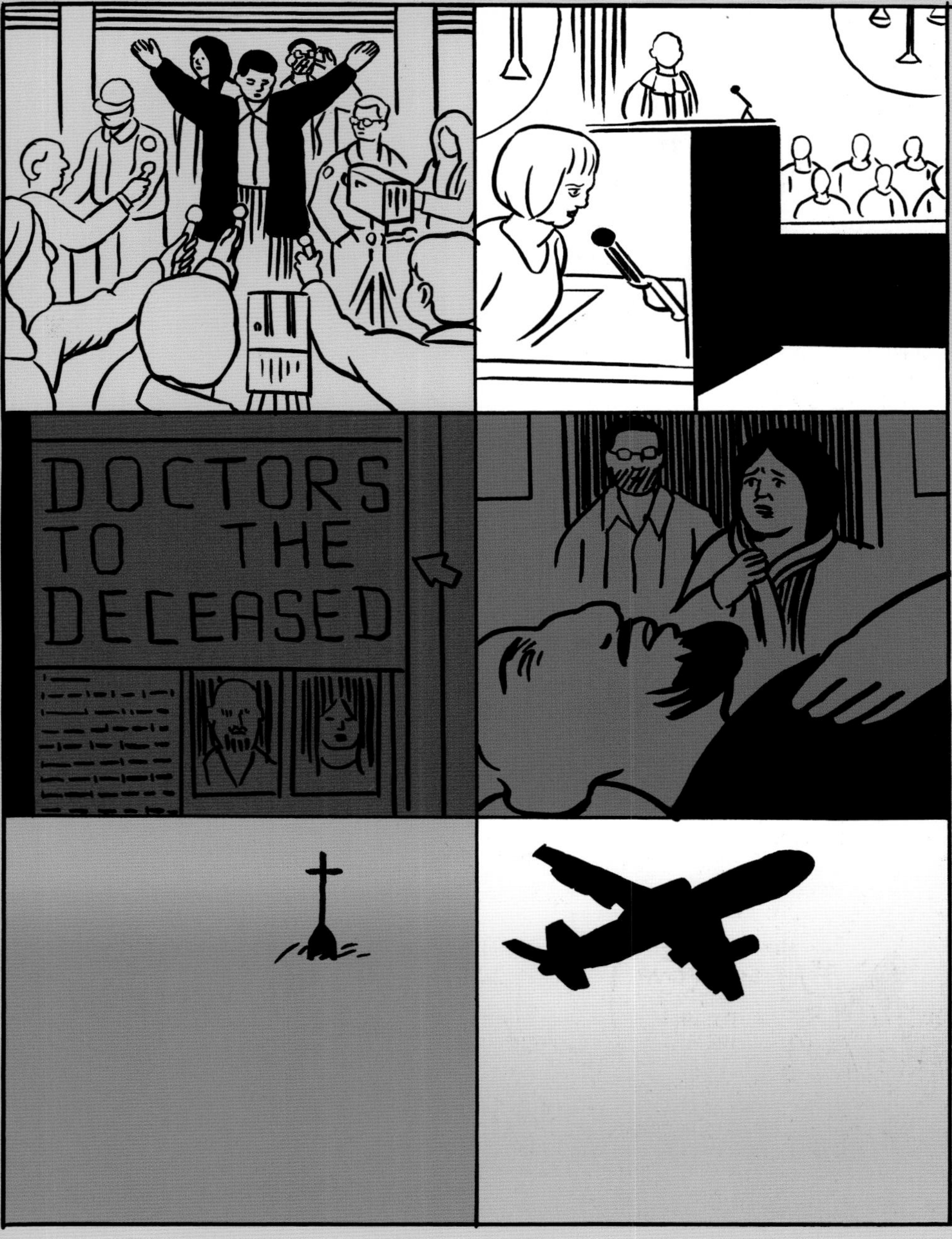
DOCTORS TO THE DECEASED

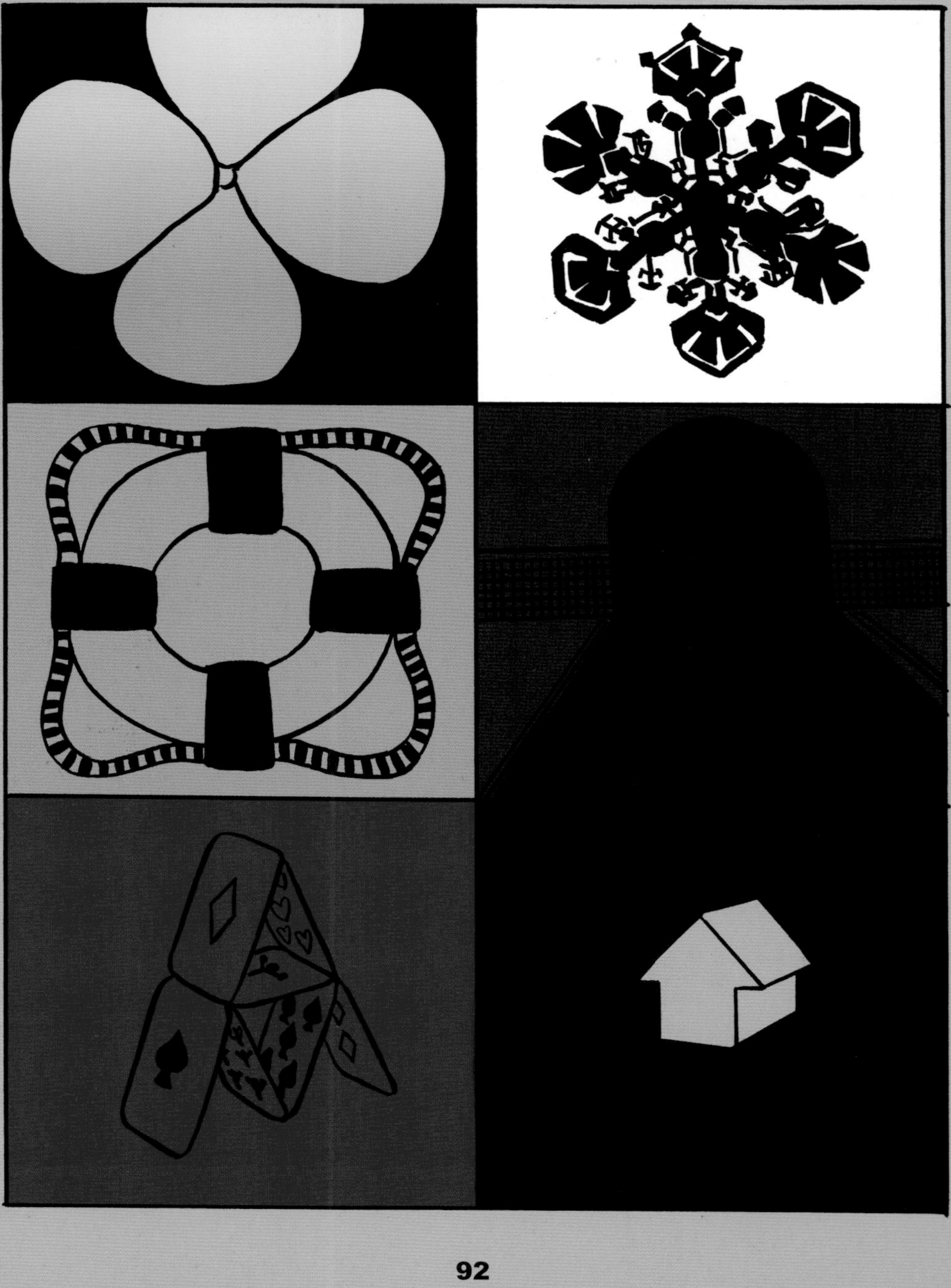

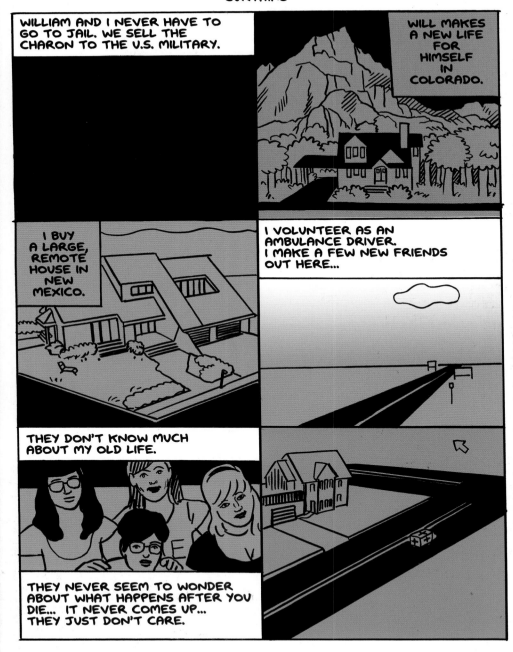

WILLIAM AND I NEVER HAVE TO GO TO JAIL. WE SELL THE CHARON TO THE U.S. MILITARY.

WILL MAKES A NEW LIFE FOR HIMSELF IN COLORADO.

I BUY A LARGE, REMOTE HOUSE IN NEW MEXICO.

I VOLUNTEER AS AN AMBULANCE DRIVER. I MAKE A FEW NEW FRIENDS OUT HERE...

THEY DON'T KNOW MUCH ABOUT MY OLD LIFE.

THEY NEVER SEEM TO WONDER ABOUT WHAT HAPPENS AFTER YOU DIE... IT NEVER COMES UP... THEY JUST DON'T CARE.

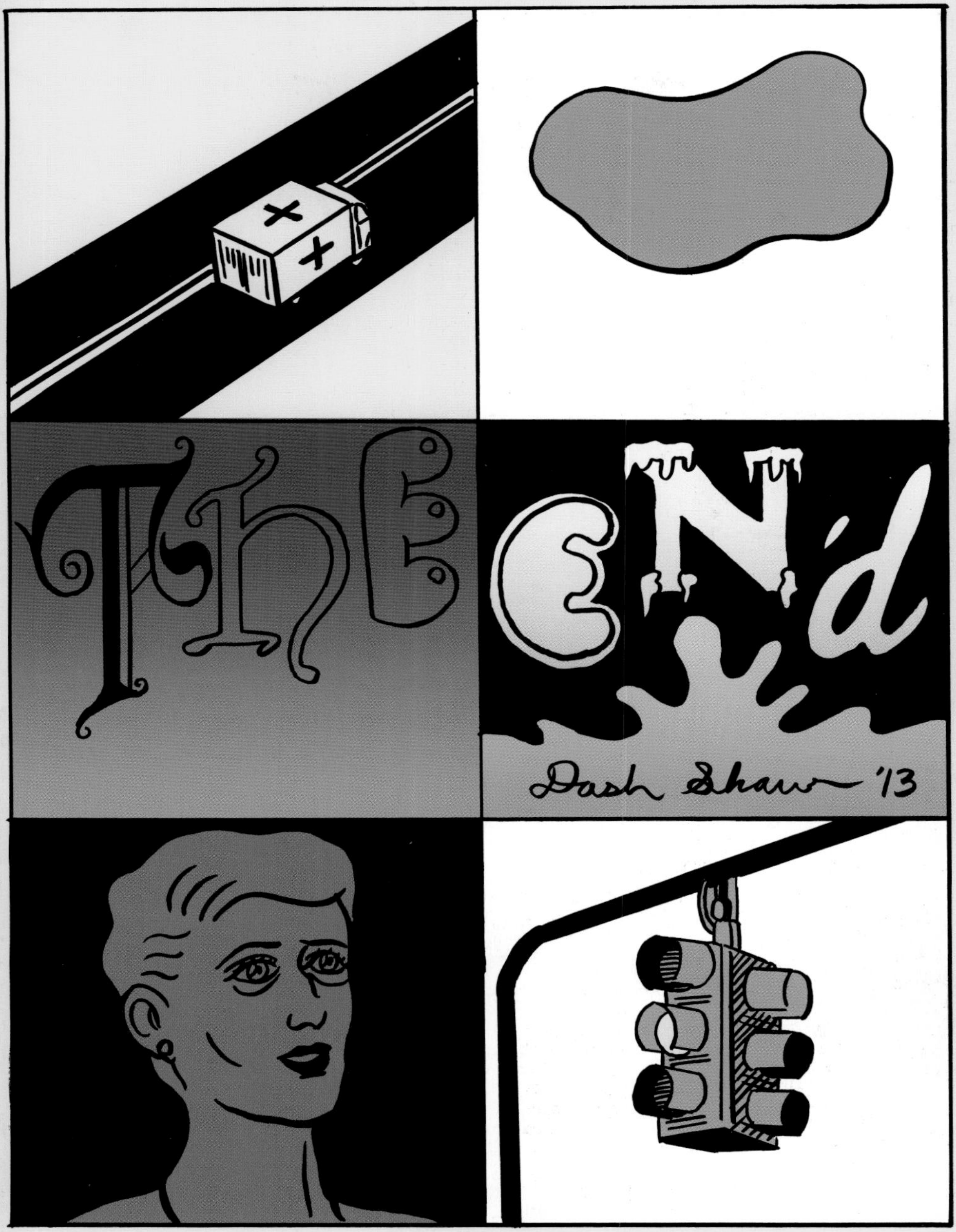
THE
END
Dash Shaw '13

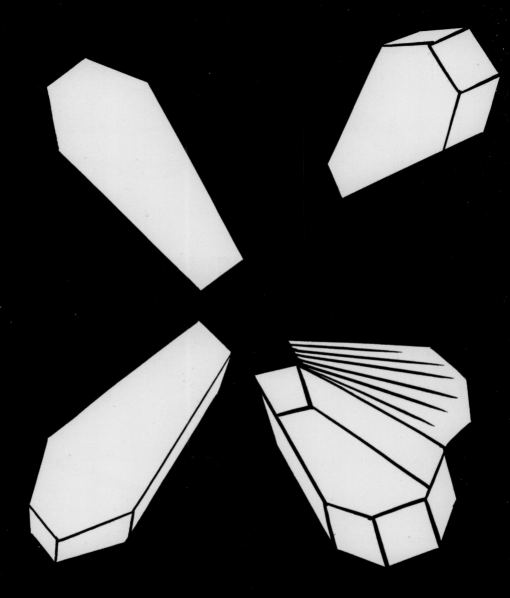

Thanks for reading.

Also by Dash Shaw:
Cosplayers, New School, 3 New Stories,
New Jobs, BodyWorld, The Unclothed Man
*in the 35th Century AD, Bottomless Belly Butto*n

dashshaw.tumblr.com